The Life of Mind

by

Paul S. Delp
Professor Emeritus of Philosophy

with an Introduction by
Dr. Cameron Sinclair
Vice President for Academic Affairs
Chapman College

Front Cover Design
by Jackie Leu Walker

Mills Publishing Company
King Station—Box 6158
Santa Ana, California 92706

THE LIFE OF MIND

Copyright ©1983 by Mills Publishing Company

ISBN: 0-935356-05-3
Library of Congress Catalog Card No.: 82-61238

Printed in The United States of America.

DEDICATION

*To the creative spirit wherever it manifests itself
and to those persons who seek its liberation.*

Blessings,

Paul Delp

PREFACE

Since my autobiography *"All the Days,"* which I intended as my last writing, I have become increasingly fascinated with the life of mind. The wellspring of ideas keeps bubbling up out of the subconscious or whatever.

So this work not only considers the historical aspect of mind but speculates on more recent discoveries in areas of the brain. The left hemisphere's function of logic, computing and reasoning complements the right hemisphere's intuition and imaging. Overemphasis of the first makes for excessive criticism which weakens the function of the creative imagination.

The solution to this imbalance seems to be encouraging the creation of new answers to the exacerbating social and political problems which threaten humanity. Appreciation oils the creative process, criticism throws a monkey wrench at it.

There is an ethical aspect in this. If the critical person *intends* to be obstructing the creative person, the latter senses it and may retreat. However, criticism can be considerate and the good of the creator intended. Just so, also the appreciative work can be genuine and helpful, or merely hypocrisy, intended to curry favor. It is for the reader to judge our thesis and its usefulness.

It remains to express my personal appreciation to Dean Sinclair for his magnanimous introduction and Mrs. Ruth Bloomster for a beautiful job of typing the manuscript. Dr. Dorothy Mills has given valuable counsel in the publication.

CONTENTS

Preface

Introduction

   I The Story of Mind   11

  II Escape to Reality   35

 III The Inversion of Values   47

 IV The Origins of Creativity   63

  V Life of the Spirit   79

 VI The Task of Philosophers   97

VII The Compulsion of the Muse   103

INTRODUCTION

The following pages are an invitation to a journey and a conversation with Paul Delp. It is a journey, because it ranges broadly over space and time not only in topics and interests but also in persons from all times the world over who have cared deeply and spoken eloquently about those central issues of life and meaning. The book is studded with gems of wisdom and insight carefully selected for the journeyman who seeks guidance in living life at its best.

It is also like a conversation with Paul because those questions and values which have dominated his thinking so clearly underlie the discussion everywhere. Whatever the topic, one knows immediately that he is in touch with the very essence of Paul's deepest concerns. Beneath its more formal structure is a kind of "stream of consciousness" moving from one idea or concern to another.

The richness and diversity of these ideas and concerns are impressive, touching the character of mind, the nature of mankind, of theory and scientific discovery, how life's problems may be solved and people changed, the role of education and of the teacher, reflections on meaning and happiness, on war and prejudice and a host of other issues.

The character of this journey may be illustrated by a few examples. First, Paul affirms that "the human species is basically good as children of God," and so he rejects the notions of original sin, of pessimism and of determinism, quoting Laotzu as saying, "I find good people and bad people good, if I am good enough." If this is so, then it follows that people need education, guidance, and an opportunity to use their creative mind to contribute to the general good.

As Erasmus put it, "Is it not clear that nature or God created man not for war, but for friendship, not for destruction but for preservation, mutual aid, love, laughter, and tears for pity? He planted deep in his heart a spark of the mind of God, an image of Himself, an earthy duty to provide well-being for all." It would follow then that the person most highly evolved is one who is not oriented toward basic self-need but rather toward going beyond self, toward altruism and dedication to a cause.

For this reason Paul rejects forms of treatment in which a client is treated like a machine. If one is regarded in this way, he may lose his self-respect and further damage may result. He believes clients are to be trusted, and the therapist's role is helping the client to cure himself.

Paul's views about education reflect these same assumptions: "The teacher is only the midwife of ideas encouraging the birth of the student's own creativity.

The best criticism is self-criticism. A college student really graduates when he can deal with faults not just by criticism, but by identifying himself with them."

Paul reminds us that Einstein, Osler and Paderewski were all expelled from school; Edison stood at the bottom of his class and Lincoln "showed no promise in education," a dramatic reminder that education must come to grips more adequately with understanding and addressing man according to his true nature.

Paul quotes Alfred North Whitehead as saying, "Celibacy does not suit a university. Learning must mate itself with action." In Peace Studies, peace action may be a form of 'peace education'."

Finally Paul reflects candidly and touchingly on the time of life he has now entered. He tells us first about those special days of fall when leaves have turned golden brown, and the sun is still warm. "I am suddenly aware of Indian Summer in my own days; the slower pace as I withdraw gradually from the academic merry-go-round is welcome. There is more time to pause and listen to a bird sing, pat a stray dog, breathe deeply near a rose garden or an orange grove. The pleasure of good food tastefully prepared, and reading a book for sheer curiosity not just class preparation, make the season more delightful."

St. John of the Cross said, "In the evening of our life, we shall be judged by how we loved." It is clear from this book that Paul Delp has loved deeply, both people and ideas. If you take this journey with Paul and engage him in this conversation, you too will surely care more deeply about people and reflect more passionately on ideas that mould our lives.

Cameron Sinclair
June 1, 1982

I

The Story of Mind

The story of mind is a fascinating one. As human beings used their minds to think about mind, some amazing and myriad ideas appeared. All of which seems to attest its creativity.

For example, one of the earliest of these imaginative concepts was that of Anaxagoras, living about 500-430 B.C., the first philosopher to become known as a teacher in Athens. Perhaps Socrates heard him and was inspired by his courage in declaring the sun was not a God but hot molten rock (for which he was banished). Anaxagoras said mind was only finer atoms of matter, or seeds which animate matter. This concept was later developed by Aristotle in his naturalism.

How could smaller particles move larger? Anaxagoras says, "Mind because of its exceptional fineness and purity has knowledge of all that is, and herein it has the greatest power. Mind exists perpetually not only in things that exist, but in those that are in process of becoming." Anaxagoras is thus ambivalent. At times, a materialist, he is then forced by logic to accept dualism, mind as separate as well as immanent in matter. Parmenides said the way of truth is the unitary mind, and the way of opinion is diverse and changing senses. (475 B.C.)

Just as there was an equivocal refinement of matter into mind so the next step in the concept of mind is taken by Plato (428-348 B.C.). He solves the mind-matter problem thus. Mind is the *real*, and matter just *appearance*. The function of mind is to recollect. It has recourse to infinite knowledge.

When the artist creates, he has within himself all of the idea (mind) necessary for a masterpiece. It is the physical ability, the skill to copy the idea that hampers him. The product then must be judged not by what it seems *(appearance)* but what it is *(reality)*. Plato himself is an example of the best. Mind, soul, and spirit were the same for Plato; they were immortal.

Next in the story of mind is Aristotle (384-322 B.C.). His tribute to Plato, his teacher, was "He is as great as his ideal." Plato's tribute to him is "Aristotle needs a check rein, never a spur." Aristotle quoted Anaxagoras, "It is impossible that any form *(mind)* should exist when everything was mixed together." This is the key to Aristotle's criticism to Plato. It seems mind *appears* out of matter yet controls it. It does not undergo change as does matter. For Aristotle mind (or *form*) is this unchanging, the actual. Matter is potential. It changes and grows by mind's direction. But Aristotle does not introduce an immortality in this unchanging. He is the scientist merely *observing* life. Mind is that which *animated* the body. Life is mind, and mind is life. He does not say, but may mean, that where life dies, the mind dies.

Plotinus (205-270 A.D.) conceived a world mind, a unified idea of Plato and Aristotle. Through use of the person's undivided mind, he is able to attain union with and thus become a part of the Eternal (immortal), "The humblest particle of dust glows faintly with deity," and again—"Mind permeates matter like water does a net." The individual mind had originally emanated from world mind.

By some curious stroke of fate, the church selected Aristotle instead of Plato to confirm its theology. Thus Aquinas (1227-1274 A.D.) wrote volumes trying to square the two in dogmatics. The dark ages were the ages of contemplation, not science.

With the Renaissance the problem of mind and body was again addressed. René Descartes (1596-1650), through an amazing guess, said they interacted through the pineal gland. Perhaps this presaged the importance of endocrinology. Geulincx (1624-1669), a little later, reintroduced God in the process saying mind and body worked on parallel lines with the divine interceding occasionally to see that all was well. Thomas Hobbes (1588-1679) said that consciousness *(mind)* was merely a "jarring of the nervous system," practically eliminating the idea of mind altogether.

Benedict Spinoza (1632-1677) solved the issue by saying mind and body were two aspects of the same indeterminate entity.

John Locke (1632-1704) brought the next advance, one which has proven so durable that a modern school is based on it **(Behaviorism)**. Locke said the mind is like a blank tablet on which our myriad experiences write. The mind is *impressionable* and passive. This provided a way of *conditioning* the individual by controlling the environment as a source of experiences. It was a whole new front for educators, today quite popular.

One of the most creative insights was brought to the problem by Gottfried Leibnitz (1646-1715) in his theory of *monads*. Instead of material atoms, these were spiritual centers composing the whole universe. The pluralism was also evolving from simple to complex, from physical to plant, to animal forms. God was the supreme *monad*. Everything was animated by these mind atoms. He refuted Locke's idea that all knowledge comes from senses.

George Berkeley (1685-1753) went to subjective idealism. **Being** was in the perceiving. Things had no existence apart from *perceiving* minds, when they were not the object of perception. God was the eternal percipient sustaining the material order of the universe.

David Hume (1711-1816) reversed Berkeley saying, "Whenever I enter most intimately into myself, all I get is a sensation!" Mind or consciousness had no existence; only a series of sensations comprised experience.

This radical position served as a springboard for Immanual Kant (1724-1805), the most creative thinker since Plato. He was introspective, making the most complete analysis of his own mental process. For Kant, the reason Hume denies the existence of Mind was his failure to realize its form, its structure. Sensations were only possible when there was a structure to sustain them. This, Kant called the *a-priori*, the given. These logical intuitions, prior to experience, he listed as space and time, the limited and unlimited, the one and the many, permanence and change, the potential and actual, reality and appearance, the moment and eternal.

Just as Locke was the antecedent of behaviorism in modern psychology, so Kant was the basis for modern Gestalt psychology. For Kant, the mind was active, not passive as for Locke. There could be no sensation without intuition. For example, we might say a camera can take a picture of anything but itself. Experience is not just a succession of pictures (sensations). They require a camera to actively take the pictures. The camera is the mind which chooses and registers the objects.

Kant read the English philosophers in his constructive response, so he needed dialog with constructive criticism of his work. Albert Schweitzer, authority on the music of Bach, theologian, and African medical missionary, wrote one of his doctoral theses on Kant and was influenced by him. As the modern psychologist, D.O. Hebb writes, "A good theory is one that holds together long enough to get you a better one." Kant had no laboratory but introspection; no one to test and correct his analysis.

But he did inspire two modern schools, **Gestalt** and **Freud** who used analysis first by free association of his patients. He interpreted it by his own experience which was just what Kant had done in self-analysis. So our story of the mind brings us to the modern "science of the psyche."

Historic Concepts of Mind

1. Geulincx (1628-1669) Occasionalism—God adjusts on occasion.

2. Spinoza (1632-1677) **Double aspect**

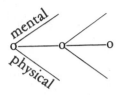

3. Locke (1632-1764)

"Tabula rasa"

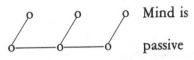

4. Leibnitz (1646-1715) preestablished harmony of Monads (spiritual atoms)

o	God
ooo	persons
oooo	animals
ooooo	plants

5. Berkeley (1685-1753)

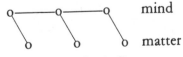

(objects not independent of mind)

6. Hume (1711-1776) Epiphenomenalism

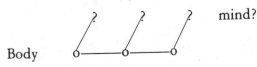

7. Kant (1724-1805

A Creative Attempt to Clarify this Complex Philosopher

Source	Kant's Correction	
	Transcendental self (Subjective)	

1) **Locke** (1632
Mind is passive.
	Mind is active.
	No percept without
	    concept (no sensation
	    without intuition)	

2) **Berkeley** (1685)
Objects exist—
    only if
    perceived.
	Objects have an existence of their own.	

3) **Hume** (1711) Mind does not exist- only sensations. (Skepticism)	Categories of mind- **a priori** intuitions Space Limited-Democritus Unlimited-Anaximander	Time Permanence-Parmenides Change-Heraclitus (Relations)

	One-Monism, Thales
	                    Spinoza
	Many-pluralism
	(Quantity) Empedocles
	                    Leibnitz
		Potential
		Actual Aristotle
		(Modality)

	Reality Appearance Plato (Quality)	Moment Eternity

Empirical self (Objective)

4) **Aquinas** (1227) **Aristotle**	God is unknowable but is postulated as base of moral feeling of "ought to," of obligation. (Not a sensation or desire). We must act as we relate to *other selves* in Freedom.
1. Cosmos requires a creator.	
2. Idea requires a Being-God (Anselm 1033)	
3. Purpose requires a purposer.	
5) **Socrates-(Plato)** (470 B.C.) Don't do what spirit says not to do (Negative conscience).	1. Act so that your act might become universal law (Essay on perpetual peace). 2. Use humanity in other selves as ends never as means (intention not results). *All* are immortal.

The first laboratories were established at Leipzig by William Wundt (1832-1920) a structuralist following Kant's contribution, and by William James (1832-1910) at Harvard in 1879. James brought Munsterburg from Germany to preside over the laboratory at Harvard, but he lost interest and joined the theorists. Wundt's pupil, Edward Titchener (1867-1927), brought the structuralist idea to Cornell, and for a time it was *structuralism* vs. *functionalism*. I remember our text in 1925 was written by Titchener. James was far more attractive and readable, although he himself said it was a pot boiler turned out to make money at the urging of his publishers!

A more promising development than the work of the laboratories at Harvard and Leipzig was the beginning of testing abilities of the mind by Alfred Binet (1905) in Paris and the American revision and adaptation of his testing of children by Lewis Terman of Stanford. They were trying to find a common factor to measure intelligence, mental ability. There were serious questions raised when many school systems adopted them in order to classify students as gifted, average, or subaverage. The *I.Q. Concept* was the work of William Stern at University of Berlin.

I had personal experience of these questions when doing public school testing in Edinburgh (1930) with Dr. Mary Collins at the University. Dr. James Drever taught History of Psychology. The Scottish Universities were more favorable to psychology than the British, which were still influenced by Green's opposition at Oxford as an idealist of the Hegelian type, although McDougall had founded the *hormic school* there. Sir Percy Nunn at **London Training School** for teachers followed this *hormic* or instinctive type. I found him an excellent teacher of teachers (1931) and enjoyed his book, *Education: Its Data and First Principles*. I also interviewed Sir Cyril Burt who wrote *The Young Delinquent*. He had taken his degree at Oxford under McDougall (1871-1938) who recommended him because of his interest in measurement of children's abilities. He knew Sir Francis Galton and used his typology in his classification. He followed Spearman over at University College where he retired (1932). I lived across the street from the college and heard Pryns Hopkins and J.C. Flugel, colleagues of Burt there. Spearman worked in factor theory and found a general factor of intelligence in 1904, similar to Terman's testing, but later isolated specific factors which seemed to me a more sensible modification. Burt was criticized before his death for studies showing a racial base of intelligence as inborn and 80% inherited. Beth Wellman at the University of Iowa found intelligence largely modified by environment.

James' interest had turned from the laboratory and attempts at measurement to psychical research as a more fruitful field of study. He said, ''Most people live physically, intellectually and morally in a restricted circle of their potential, a small portion of their soul's resources, like a man who gets in the habit of using only his little finger. Psychical research is a field in which deception is possible. But there is no source of deception comparable to the fixed belief that certain kinds of phenomena are not possible.''

Edwin D. Starbuck of the University of Southern California preceded James in Psychology of Religious Phenomena studies. I was impressed by his careful reverent yet scientific approach in my contact with him.

Of all places he found support from the physicist who would be thought to adhere religiously to the method of physics. Steinmetz, the electrical wizard, said, ''The greatest discovery will be made along spiritual lines. Material things are of little use in making persons creative. When scientists study spiritual forces, the world will see more advancement in one generation then the past four.''

And the great Einstein said, ''The fairest thing we can experience is the mysterious. It is the cradle of true art and science.'' His friend Hans Reichenbach asked him how he discovered the theory of relativity. He replied, ''Because I was so strongly convinced of the harmony of the universe.''

I knew Reichenbach after he came to UCLA from Berlin. I invited him to Chapman where he spoke in an Assembly. I used his text, *Experience and Prediction*, in Epistemology, but his most famous book was *The Rise of Scientific*

Philosophy. One of his statements is a classic in support of the thesis of this book, "The critical attitude may make man incapable of discovery. The creative physicist may prefer his creed to the logic of the analytic philosopher." (My thesis, *appreciation* is more significant than *criticism* for creative mind.)

Bertrand Russell gives the way to develop a creative idea. "A theory *must not emerge* from a careful collection of individual observations (scientific method). It must emerge as a sudden *imaginative insight.*"

Arnold Toynbee, the historian, stresses this by writing, "To give a chance to potential creativity is a matter of life and death for any society."

With this support from science, philosophy, and history, we continue to consider the psychologists. J.P. Guilford (1897-) of the University of Southern California uses a structure approach. The mind's operations are cognition, memory, convergent and divergent thinking, and evaluation. There is no relation of creativity to intelligence. Guilford developed a multiple factor theory of intelligence as Spearman had done.

I believe the life of the mind is the conscious will to create **(appreciation)**. The death of the mind is the conscious will to destroy **(criticism)**. Perhaps we create our own immortality in this way by creative ideas. Our eternal life consists in creating ideas. Good ideas are those which survive the test of time. Bad ideas do not need criticism to die but perish of their own accord.

The most creative idea next in the story of mind was that of Sigmund Freud (1856-1939). James had pictured mind as "the stream of consciousness," but this was too pretty a picture for Freud who was concerned with the *illnesses of the mind*. He observed two patients in adjacent hospital beds with the same diagnosis and given the same treatment, one survived and the other died. There must be some other cause than chemical. He got his clue from Schopenhauer who wrote, "Can man evolve consciousness great enough to overcome his problems before the unconscious destroys us?"* The conscious points to the

---

*Schopenhauer, Arthur. *The World as Will and Idea.* [*Will* is the subconscious, the source of creativity in art.]

future and immortality of super conscious, the unconscious to the past.

Freud took these three parts, calling them *Ego, Superego,* and *Id.* Freud saw the *Id* as the unconscious, the heritage of long centuries of evolution, the will to live, and with it the will to conflict, even to kill. This was the answer to the unresolved questions of consciousness. But there was an ambivalence in it, for it also harbored the death urge for itself as well as others in the struggle. He used Greek drama to name his findings, **Oedipus** and **Electra.**

Freud was a pessimist—death is the winner. His antipathy for religion made the idea of immortality repugnant. Freud was also a determinist. There was no escaping doom. Even in his morose answer he sought escape and found it in the *libido*; love finds a pseudo-immortality in our children. (See Freud—*Future of an Illusion.*)

The ego was conscious self. The **super-ego** was the imposition of society, particularly parents and teachers, who dominated the *ego.* Thus the *ego* was crushed between the *id* and *super-ego.* While Arthur Schopenhauer in his pessimism had given the aces to the unconscious, he held a way of escape through the superconscious which was a *development,* a growth in the conscious, a possibility of immortality. It is significant that Freud near the end of his life said that if he had a chance to live his life over, he would devote it to psychical research! Gordon Allport said of him, "He ploughed, but he didn't plant." The psychoanalyst, Bruno Bettelheim, maintains that Freud's German writing has been misinterpreted in the English translations in the United States. He feels they are attempts to make him subject to medical scientific interpretations which lose much of the intuitive and emotional aspects. Freud had said, "Psychoanalysis is the application of love to healing." Goethe, the German poet, was his favorite. Bettelheim regards Freud's German as poetic.

Freud's pioneer work spawned a number of developments in his students. Each had to be psychoanalyzed by Freud, and thus he kept his monopoly on the idea of mind he advocated. Alfred Adler (1870-1937) stressed the will to power, the courage to overcome handicaps, creative life style, mental health. He emphasized the social aspects conceiving the inferiority and superiority complexes as resulting from inadequacy or success in the group contacts. I heard Adler lecture in 1928 and was impressed with the inclusiveness of his thought after the selectivity of Freud's approach.

Carl Jung (1875-1961) took a more religious than social tangent from Freud. He added the concepts of introversion and extroversion to the vocabulary as well as a mythology of spirits. Analyst Hans Eysenck found no one method of psychoanalysis superior.

I find much thought stimulation in Freud, as did his pupils. His use of Greek drama is particularly significant. Just as he modified Schopenhauer's three elements, so I would like to suggest a rearrangement of his three, *id, ego,* and *superego,* which seems to me closer to the truth. Freud's fear of the spiritual led him to place his *superego* in the social environment. Conscience was *a posteriori,* after the fact of the individual's existence. For me *conscience* is more basic than the *id.* (See next essay, **The Real Center.**) This is a philosophic position which I hypothesize with as much reason as does Freud. The test is will experience prove it is better? The basis is a disagreement over the nature of a person. Freud stacks the cards finding the human evil. I believe that facts will show he is basically good. I do not believe in original sin. The person is a child of God. What happens is that we treat people differently according to our belief. If evil, they need control restrictions, power by force over them.

Nothing is said about the one exerting the force, dictating, restricting. He seems to be assumed to be without sin! On the other hand if the person is basically good, he needs *educating* (the Latin meaning is *instructive—to lead out)* guidance, yes, but the chance to contribute his essential creative mind to the general good. I am not a pessimist or determinist. Creativity in each person may or may not succeed in every case, but there is a good chance. In Freud's theory a person can't be forced to be creative.

The other development from Kant's work was the Gestalt with

Max Wertheimer (1880-1943), and Kohler (1887-1967) as pioneers. They took the categories of Kant's self-analysis and found in their studies of perception that the individual sees in whole, meaningful objects, not elements or parts. Our minds have this given by nature as they see relationships.

While these European ideas of mind were developing, American progress came in **behaviorism**. John B. Watson (1878-1958) at Johns Hopkins University was experimenting with conditioning, a work inspired by Pavlov's pioneer work with dogs. I was in awe of Knight Dunlap when taking his course on Habit Formation at U.S.C. This man had worked with Howison, the personalist, at U.C. Berkeley, Munsterberg, James and McDougall at Harvard, and Watson at Johns Hopkins. More recently B.F. Skinner (1904-) of Harvard enthused about creating a new society through conditioning in education. *Biofeedback* has shown good results in adjustment therapy. Mr. Ray Wingard, a student of mine in History and Systems of Psychology, had correspondence with Skinner on the "Skinner Box" concept. Skinner was forthcoming with detailed handwritten information and comments. Psychiatry Professor Judd Marmor suggests combining behaviorist and psychoanalytic techniques.

Behaviorism has been blurred by various modifications from S — R (stimulus-response) to S — O — R (organism changes) to $S — O — R^1 R^2$, etc. (different responses by the same organism.)

The last development in the life of mind is that of the humanists. A reaction in this country set in to the determinism of psychoanalysis, its extended length of therapy with attendant costs, and the mechanical treatment of the behaviorists with its reductionism.

Carl Rogers (1902-) wrote, "The reason so much experimentation is done on rats and cats is that we realize we don't have the tools for understanding human beings." He conceived a non-directive therapy, *just listening* to patients. Freud has done this in free association but interjected questions which Rogers felt tended to make the patient try to conform to Freud's direction. Rogers believed the patient would find his own answers as he ruminated. Here we see a new attitude toward the patient. He is *to be trusted,* and he helps cure himself.

Gordon Allport (1897-1967) at Harvard stressed the importance of the whole person. His colleague, Murray, says of him, "He was courteous, considerate, stressing goals relating to self respect, individual as unique. He was antipathetic to drives, emotions, and situational determinants" as contrasted to Freud and Watson. He had a notable list of students particularly effective in teaching creativity (McKinnon, Barron and Erickson).

I wrote to him in 1939 for suggestions on an introductory text. Characteristically, he suggested biography was the best way for beginning students to get the vision of what the study of mind could give.

H.A. Murray (1893-) himself made a major contribution in his thematic perception test. He created a series of pictures for boys, girls, men and women. The person, as each picture is shown, is asked to tell a story about it. Rorschalk used ink blots for the same purpose. The problem, of course, is that each instructor may interpret the stories differently. At least it is an attempt to get the individual activity of the creative mind, not just a standardized test.

Abraham Maslow (1908-1970) finds that the person has certain peak and plateau experiences. He is holistic in approach, accepting a transcendent nature. He criticizes much of the scientific method as reductionist and value free. "The ultimate disease of our time is valuelessness." He advocates a discussion of values which emphasizes what a person may become, not just testing as he is. The more highly evolved person is not basic self-need oriented but beyond self, altruistic, dedicated to a cause.

In the *Life of Mind,* we conclude that its future development will be interdisciplinary, touching its basis in philosophy, its social and cultural setting, and in concern for life of the spirit. This brief introduction may provide a background for what follows. In **The Real Center, The Growth of Creative Conscience, Periodic Maturity, The Development of the Hap-**

py Life, and **The Death Urge**, we shall be considering critical
and creative ideas from Freud's theory. **The Psychology of Adjustment** and **Reflex and Reflection** are critical of behavior
theory.

The author's theory is personalist or humanist, and the critiques of Freud and **behaviorism** are from that point of view.

The Real Center
*Labor to keep alive in your heart that little spark
of celestial fire, conscience*
—George Washington.

What then is the real center of our existence? It is the incorruptible conscience. It is deeper than the *id* of Freud. Freud as
a true artist came close to the heart of reality with his
penetrating analogies of *id, ego,* and *superego.* The *id* was the
will to live at all cost. The *ego* was the apparent individual (the
iceberg above water, as the *id* was the unseen part below.) The
superego was society, custom, which imposes control on the individual, often against his will *(id)* causing all manner of
frustrations and abnormality.

Freud's keen insight brought many amazing cures. His
pupils, Adler and Jung, continued the discoveries with Adler's
interpretation of the *will to power* and its consequent
superiority and inferiority complexes, and Jung's emphasis on
faith and the inner life. But these were built on Freud's concept of the *id.*

What if there were a something deeper than the *id!* It is conceivable that Freud did not penetrate all the way. It is possible
that there was a "beyond that was within." It is conceivable
that the final word does not rest with the will to survive at all
costs, to kill and conquer.

Perhaps Freud's error was in identifying *conscience* with the
superego. * He did not look long enough at the *superego* he
had conceived. If he had, he would have been disappointed in
failing to discover the *conscience.* He assumed that our consciences are the result of custom and training, and, when we
get in a new situation, our former training says, "no" and this

---

* Freud wrote, "Conscience originates from dread of the community and nothing
else."

is *conscience!* He fell into the behavioristic net of *conditioning* as the determinant.

Conscience is *sui generis.* It is the uncreated nature of the individual. This is the actual nature, the real center. Not to realize it in our lives is not to have lived. That is what is meant by the tragedy of all tragedies; for the artist, it is to die with his picture unpainted.

If this real self were the product of education and training, it would be easy to create character. The task of Pygmalion in creating Galatea would have been so simple we would never have heard the story. The reason it is great is that it failed; it was tragedy. Too, it's no good to ape society. That is to become artificial and something less than natural.*

No, conscience is not to be confused with the *superego.*

Now the only way we are God-like is in our conscience, the real center. Conscience is perfect; it is a God atom. But our consciences may be frustrated by our desires, just as our desires may be frustrated by our *superego* (society), and so we miss the perfect life. Buddha saw deeper into man than Freud at this point, but his answer was impossible to achieve, namely, the elimination of desire.

It would be just as impossible to eliminate the *id* as eliminate conscience; desire cannot be eliminated as long as there is life. Plato's answer was more realistic. He spoke of the dilemma in terms of two horses, a black unruly one, and a gentle, tractable white one. The good man did not eliminate either desires or wisdom from his nature but made them pull together.

But conscience is not to be confused with wisdom either, any more than with society, past or present. Wisdom is sagacity, the application of intelligence to situations. It presumes an adjustment to certain situations in order to overcome them. It is a

---

*Similarly, we may sometimes confuse the voice of desires, impulses, for the voice of conscience, the will to give. An example of this would be the Inquisition, which may have been *conscientiously* administered by at least some of the church authorities, but, in truth, the *"id"* in each of them facilitated their reactions. The conscience is always personal, never general.

pragmatic quality, an end in view.*

Conscience is not like this. It is like Job saying to God: "Though He slay me, yet will I trust Him!" We can become like God, perfect in good will, as we give way to the inner light, the voice of conscience. We do it, not by eliminating desire (Buddha's way), nor by sublimating it (a la Freud), but by penetrating it.

The *id* is only formidable when we leave it whole and assume it is ultimate. A parallel can be drawn to the history of physics, with its certainty that it had reached the ultimate in the molecule, only to discover the atom, and then the electron. Heisenberg and Einstein penetrated further in theory. Just so, conscience is theory, but upon that theory can be founded structure for the human sphere.

Over fifty years ago, I had a professor in psychology who ridiculed Freud. He would ask members of the class if they knew where their subconscious was. He would point to the base of the head, the back of the neck, pretending to localize it. No one had ever seen a "subconscious" in brain operations. Why assume its existence?

But Freud's assumption answered certain questions and thus was practical. William James, certainly no Freudian with this emphasis on consciousness, had found acting "as if" something were true might initiate its reality, thus bringing it into being.

So it may be that the concept of conscience, "The taproot of God," as Rufus Jones, Haverford psychologist and philosopher, wrote, might begin a development of the ethical sense needed in our regard and treatment of others.

A good example of the loyalty to his conscience is that of Raymond B. Cattell, head of the Department of Psychology at Columbia University, who was fired for being a pacifist in World War II.

---

*There is, however, an intellectual capacity in conscience. It *knows* by its very nature. There is an "illumination" about its work as it centers its searchlight on its environs and thereby judges the right and wrong of situations.

The Growth of Creative Conscience

How does the creative process develop? Each child is unique, so it is essential that uniqueness not be destroyed in the need for family and social conformity. This conformity, after all, can protect the child from self-destruction. The problem is to preserve the rules which the family and society have evolved from bitter experience and yet allow the child to develop the talent from the depth of his own conscience. It is this talent, which if fostered, that may eventually change that society for the better.

What are these stages of growth? First the **no-no** stage. The mother is the giantess of the nursery whose sheer size demands assent. As psychologists tell us, there is a negative period (age 2 to 4 years) during which each child tries to assert his uniqueness. How the parent handles this is the solution. It is his or her first chance to begin self-discipline. For example, if the child's attention span, which is very short now, can be redirected to some acceptable object or activity, the process of choosing is begun for the child. His energy flows where there is least resistance like water.

The second period is the **legalistic,** the law observance. In primitive society it is **the taboo.** Certain activities just aren't done. No particular reasoning is attached because they are regarded as either right or wrong. The pre-adolescent is in this "cowboy and Indian" era, the good guys and the bad guys. The law and order advocates may be examples of this blind acceptance. Many adults never graduate from this stage. They see all moral situations as either black or white.

The third is the **Golden Rule stage.** Treat others as you want them to treat you. Here there is agreement reached between youth, a negotiating process so that each agrees to consider the creativity of the other and receives like recognition in return. The youth sees that in seeking justice for all, he meets his own needs. Now the creative process has evolved from just seeking to avoid the "giantess of the nursery" and possible punishment through obeying the laws also superimposed, to the internalization of control. Self-discipline is born now if it has not been suffocated in the early stages.

The final period, full maturity, sees the person choose freely his goals and ideals in terms of an overall perspective, a world view. Many never get beyond the second period, and so the creative conscience may be realized by a limited number. There are those with the vision to change the established order to one which is more consonant with the perfect world order, and they are so endowed with creative conscience that this process will be nonviolent. Examples of such creative persons are: Schweitzer, Gandhi, Martin Luther King, and preeminently, Jesus.

Periodic Maturity

The theory of periodic maturity is that complete satisfaction in each stage of development makes for happy adjustment in the next stage. If there is frustration or trauma in any stage, it may cause maladjustment in those stages which follow.

This theory accounts for the middle age examples of frantic seeking of fulfillment. The husband who plays Don Juan or the wife who feels she is deprived and begins extra marital affairs illustrate the coming to surface of early frustration.

The most cruel form of discipline a parent can impose is withholding love. This drives the maladjustment deeper into the psyche. By giving love to the maladjusted, emotionally disturbed, and frustrated person, therapy can be achieved.

The principle of reciprocity that, if the child does something of which the parent disapproves he should be rejected, is one which works only superficially and temporarily. It gets immediate results but causes hidden problems which cannot be released except by acceptance and love.

The same therapy is needed in the adult as in the child. If he can't find love in acceptable ways, he seeks it in non-acceptable terms of society's standards. Love is the specific for problems arising from its lack in earlier stages.

Too often the emotionally disturbed are avoided as having a personal devil. But avoiding the ill allows fear to develop in the avoider which is a source of mental illness.

The Development of the Happy Life

I believe the happy life is one which has experienced complete satisfaction in each stage of maturing. The child who has not had complete satisfaction being nourished at its mother's breast as a baby cannot be in a state of readiness for childhood. He is fixated and constantly regresses to infancy.

Just so, the youth who has not experienced the completion of childhood returns to it with a nostalgia that is overwhelming. He is fixated in *narcissism* because he has not lived through it completely at the proper stage of his development.

Aristotle was not far from the truth in saying that happiness is to realize our potentialities. There are prepotencies in everyone, which, if not brought to fruition, leave one in the tragic position of facing death having left his song unsung, and we are all the poorer for it. *Happiness is the fortunate concurrence of these potencies and circumstances, at each stage of human development.*

The Death Urge

Freud pointed out the significance of the death urge in understanding abnormal behavior.

But the death urge has a place in living. How else could we rid ourselves of those things in life which are harmful to the abundant life? This urge is actually good for some characteristics and qualities: we have to die that a better person may live, figuratively speaking. Freud pointed to the *ego* as the object of an ongoing struggle between the *id* (instinctive drives) and the *superego* (personal adoption of society's values). In the spiritual life, which we are to consider, the ego of self-centeredness is gradually sublimated into the other-center of God.

So we begin to see the good in what was regarded by the critics as evil. The death of a lower form is essential for the birth of a higher. The caterpillar becomes a butterfly.

The Hindu religion saw the value in death even to creating a God of destruction, Siva. Without Siva, it is said, the world would be a collosal state of putrefaction.

And this too is why Hinduism naturally adopted reincarnation. Life goes into new forms as the old dies.

Freud thought the libido life force may be violent in order to live, and he thought it was indivisible. The death urge was the ultimate winner over it. But why are they both evil? And why are they indivisible? Why isn't it possible to conceive the death urge working with the life force, and that both are good? Thus the death urge can be useful in destroying the evil rather than the good. (At times Freud seems to see them together.) It can eliminate the violent and vicious. Some forms of life such as cancer need eliminating, too.

Evil will gradually be eliminated as man achieves divinity. The scientist-priest, Tielhard du Chardin, believed man continues to evolve and will be able to achieve a level which will overcome his problems.

It is possible that the world is dying. If this theme is true, it is high time we get about the business of creating a new world. From the viewpoint of a great drama it is entirely conceivable that the springtime of the world was that Golden Day from 500 B.C. to the time of Christ with the gifts of Laotzu, Confucius, Buddha, Socrates, Plato, Aristotle, and Jesus.

Our age could be the coming of winter, and there are many indications that this is not far from the truth. Our scientific advances have not given us security or permanence. The methods of violence and destruction are practiced religiously in our international relations. The United Nations is becoming a sounding board for national jealousies. Many of our statesmen work on this false premise that violence is the answer to violence. They are aware of no alternative.

At least two responses are possible to this situation. One is to go along and accept the naturalistic hypothesis that the world has a birth, life, and death, and we are witnessing the dying agony. But even assuming this may be true, we do not need to be passive; we can help as midwives of the new life which is born even on the naturalistic theory. What is this creative task? To that we turn and give our most serious attention, for it is the most vital question of modern times. If we would live well in our day and time, then we cannot escape the creative task.

We must do something about our starving surroundings.

Man, by nature, is created to give to his environs; when he takes all and gives nothing, he is cutting off his source of supply. The bee who takes the honey pollinates the flower too.

Man is unhappy because he thinks he will attain happiness by getting, and it eludes him the more with every added possession.

Many really believe that anyone who suggests giving as the source of happiness is merely preaching. The bird who sings as if his throat would burst understands intuitively the real secret. The great tragedy, as has been said, is in the life which dies with its song still inside, unsung.

The Psychology of Adjustment

A basic course taught in many college departments of psychology is The Psychology of Adjustment. Texts are written also with that title.

The aim is to adjust the person to his physical and social environment. There are several questions of a philosophic nature which need to be raised with such a point of view.

The first is its acceptance generally, without being challenged. This indicates that psychology, which grew out of philosophy, may need to return and look again at its basic premises. What does adjustment mean?

The picture it elicits is of a machine. The mechanic adjusts the carburetor in the automobile—or the spark plugs—or the brakes. Is the person a machine? If the answer is affirmative then he may be treated like one. Shock treatments show little regard for the patient as a person. All forms of psychological and medical treatment can take on this impersonal and mechanical nature.

When the person realizes he is regarded in this manner, he may lose his self-image, his self-respect. This, in turn, leads to all forms of mistreatment.

The second question is in regard to social adjustment. This problem may be even more serious than the first. Adapting the person to the social and economic order as it is means not questioning the establishment. What if things as they are are harmful to the person?

For example, a transition belt in a factory moving along at a steady pace requires the worker to perform his specific task during the movement; then it proceeds to the next worker for his assignment. The worker has to adjust, regardless of any chance interruption. This is certainly stressful. Further, what if the belt were accelerated? This is the nature of a mechanized control threatening the person with a nervous breakdown.

Any negative changes in the economic order brings stress even to the point of suicide with those who can't adjust. The same is true with interpersonal relations.

On the other hand, adaptation to a static non-developing environment makes for conforming persons, without the challenge of self-development. René Dubos, the environmental authority, pointed out this problem.

A third question grows out of that. Are we to assume in an adjustment psychology that the environment is perfect? How do we bring about social change and progress with such an adaptation? Conforming persons are not creative. They are suitable candidates for a regimented state and a dictator.

Reflex and Reflection

In psychology the term *reflex* is used to indicate an immediate reaction to a stimulus such as an eye blink when a hand is passed quickly before the face, or a knee jerk when a doctor taps the knee with a tiny mallet.

Reflection on the other hand means there has been a period short or long between the stimulus and response when thought may take place.

In confrontation situations, the reflex act has certain problems. The boy who puts a chip on his shoulder and challenges another boy to knock it off means he will strike back at once. There is only one type of reaction. But if the stimulus is filtered through the cortex, there is the possibility of varying reactions. Choice is involved. There is still the possibility of striking back, but other alternatives may be considered which might result in a happier solution.

This is the advantage that the non-violent person has over the violent one. He has chosen a life style which is not a knee jerk. He has alternatives which may include not only self-protection but concern for the opponent and any others who might be affected by his action. By reflection he has a chance to find better answers to confrontation situations. It was Alfred N. Whitehead who wrote, "Progress of man can be summed up in the distance he has traveled from force to persuasion."

II

Escape to Reality

Much of modern psycho-therapy is concerned with getting neurotic people adjusted to "reality," roughly defined as the day and things with which we live. This is based on the assumption that our day and its trappings are all right. Psychiatrists diagnose much of mental trouble as an "escape *from* reality."

There is the alternative possibility that the world, as we experience it, is not reality. The world of appearance, with its wars, rumors of wars, competition, hate and jealousy, has much that is false and unreal in it. To say that we must adjust to it would not mean mental health, but ill health.

We need to escape *to* reality. From whence comes our salvation? By our nature we are closer to animals and plants than to mechanical contrivances, business, or trade. From the complex world of the present to the simplicity of nature is the way. Our mental health is gained and sustained by freeing ourselves from an eternal longing for something. Once we get a thing, we start wanting something else. Of course, we have become accustomed to certain comforts in modern life. But we take satisfaction in enjoying the most simple comforts, if we can't do a "back to nature." What's more, we can put ourselves in places where nature has a chance to reach our nature, where our kinship with all living things is appreciated.

The essays which follow deal with creativity: **A Lesson in Creativity, Criticism and Creativity in Colleges, Creating College Objectives, Changing our Minds, and Psychology and Human Values.**

A Lesson In Creativity

One of the most essential things we must learn if we are to be creative is to pay attention to everything in our surroundings no matter how small . . . not, of course, all at once but successively and with ample time for study. Our environment is at times overwhelming. We tend to develop a protective coating on all our senses. If we have been too coddled, we find the light too bright, the sounds too sharp, the wind too cool, the lemon too sour, the smoke too suffocating. We anaesthetize ourselves. We sleep through the days as well as the nights.

If we can be "stabbed awake" as Stevenson says, we will take more than a second glance and the process of appreciation will be initiated. We will see color, shading, line, form. We will hear new harmonies, new range, new dissonance. We will feel new spine-tingling vigor in deep breaths. We will not desire the extremes of our day: the driver who kills himself to provide thrills for spectators. The movies are flagrant examples of this extreme remedy for boredom . . . a children's matinee where excitement is piled on excitement in stupefying succession. This generating of thrills reaches a saturation point and then degenerates into the abnormal. Movies skip from cowboys and Indians to the rape of a community by a foreign enemy in war. Children come out of the theatre bug-eyed and jaded, hardly able to react to the real world about them.

The maturity of our spiritual development may be determined by what attracts our attention and the extent to which we select the highest. At Christmas time we may be so dazzled by all the bright lights that we can't appreciate the inner light, and yet it is the latter which will eventually overcome the world's darkness.

Criticism and Creativity in Colleges

Higher education is a prime example of the effect of criticism on a person's creative efforts! Both faculty and students are engaged in research, some voluntary and some assigned.

The voluntary is a labor of love in a favorite field of study. But this task of enjoyment may make it less painful, when the student can choose in a limited area, talking over the pitfalls beforehand with the instructor. His criticism ultimately means he is actually doing the creating, while the student merely transcribes his ideas.

Edward Albee, the playwriter, expressed it well, "All criticism is prejudice." The professor's criticism is from his own point of view naturally, and, if the student follows it, his work is only imitation.

An artist friend, who achieved some success in his painting of Westerns, related how he decided to have a few pupils as he approached retirement. Imagine his dismay when he found them merely imitating his technique and copying his subjects! He gave up teaching as an impossible task.

The teacher who is himself a master of the art of teaching really knows, as did Plato writing of Socrates, that he is only the midwife of ideas, encouraging the birth of the student's own creativity; he gets his satisfaction vicariously in the achievements of his students.

Some instructors tend also to transfer this concept from their students to their colleagues on the faculty and administration. They perceive the total nature of the College as one of *cooperative education.* Instead of criticism of fellow workers, in competition for students, they complement them, supplementing their own abilities where they see a lack in another's. Every member of the community of scholars has strong points, as well as weak. The successful functioning of the institution depends on this covering for each other in a particular need rather than sitting in the seat of the scorner, even trying to have someone on the staff lose his position.

The best criticism is self-criticism. The creative person, which means everyone in the College Community, is his own best evaluator. If he has survived the various and multitudinous criticisms of all kinds of teaching through the grades (itself a major achievement in creativity), he has developed self-confidence and this, together with self-respect which makes him discriminating, forms the basis for unique creation. To paraphrase G.B. Shaw, "Those that can—create, those that can't—criticize the creators." There is a kind of impotence in critical persons.

Shaw, Einstein, Osler and Paderewski were all expelled from school. Edison was at the bottom of his class, and Lincoln showed "no promise" of education.

The "conflict" theorists may criticize for not encouraging competitive ideas in finding better ways to answer social and economic problems. So it should be made clear that internecine, interpersonal cutting up between colleagues destroys the climate of freedom to propose ideas. The solution is in a discussion openly without hesitation, of all ideas, the *group* selecting possible alternatives and experimenting. The combined idea has more chance of being the right one, rather than one person's subjugating all others. Again, to use Socratic dialogue, when a number of persons work together to find the solution to a problem, the chances are better than with one alone. A good committee functions in this manner.

Discussion is best when carried on in an atmosphere of cooperation, indicated by comments such as, "Perhaps we would like to consider further . . ."; "Should we look at alternative possibilities . . ."; "Your comment reminds me that . . ." Even if one disagrees, it does not have to be open opposition. Such techniques are very important in committee work. In the most serious confrontation one should seek out the opponent at an appropriate time, perhaps over a meal, to understand one another in detail. When outcomes are considered, they usually find they both want the best answers. The total good of the College is the aim of each. To will otherwise is to ultimately injure oneself.

All members of the College Community should be involved. Maintenance suggestions are invaluable when planning new buildings or remodeling. An example would be architects' use of planters for exterior aesthetic effort, without considering the almost impossible task of maintenance, watering, etc.

Can colleges become democratic? Perhaps the extremes of the University of California at San Diego or Goddard (where the one man-one vote for all—janitors, students, faculty, staff, and president)—isn't needed. But there is need by the administration to listen to workers in their area.

Decisions on curriculum need interdisciplinary input. Someone has said trying to change a college curriculum is like trying to reorganize a cemetery. Each department has concerned itself over the years with pyramid building, competing with other departments for students, even sometimes within the department. An example of the latter comes to mind of the time another professor accused me of "stealing his students," because unknown to me, three students from his class were auditing mine.

Curriculum changes are difficult because some senior professor may have vested interests in pet courses. They use the same notes for years. One said he used notes of a course he took twenty years earlier! The incident is told of one of these "time-saving" professors who put his lectures on a recorder so he wouldn't even need to go to class. Late in the term he appeared unexpectedly to see how it was going. To his dismay he found no students but thirty recorders! R.A. Millikan, when he was president of the California Institute of Technology, advocated changing from the lecture method to problem solving in laboratory. He was a Nobel prize winner in physics.

Required courses can be another way of guaranteeing class size and insuring one's professorship. At Harvard in 1828, a third of the student body was expelled for rioting against requirements. The result was the elective system.

Of course, a certain body of knowledge is essential for advanced work in particular major fields, but studies show that most students change their major several times during their college days. Apart from the basics of communication skills, freshmen should be introduced to wide ranging interdisciplinary opportunities. Helen Keller once said, "College isn't the place to go for 'new ideas'." Perhaps, if the challenge to creative thinking were more emphasized, both faculty and students would grow intellectually.

Not only is the faculty infected with excessive competition, but so are the students by means of the grading system. If the faculty only wants to grade the creativity of students, there will be little of it. But if they set the example by their own creative work in their particular fields, the inspiration may bring a rich harvest. Evaluation can be either positive or negative.

Richard Armour writes of the desire of many students, who conform to the system of grading, seeking A + 's, which he defines as "slightly better than perfect." They are not encouraged to creativity by this method but are tempted to devious ways of attaining it.

A promising development is the use of intern programs, where the student (particularly in social sciences and business) gets a chance for learning outside the classroom. Harvard's Alfred North Whitehead wrote, "Celibacy does not suit a University. It must mate itself with action." The early universities were isolated from the community in which they were situated. The town and gown conflicts were the rule. The findings of the classroom must meet the needs of dynamic social and political order. Its influence can guide the process to a better future for the greater community which includes the university.

In teaching peace studies, for example, peace action may be one form of peace education.

Creating College Objectives

In 1971, Chapman College inaugurated a new President, Dr. Donald C. Kleckner. One of his first aims as president was to choose goals and objectives for the college. Accordingly he approved a committee on goals, with three from the Administration: Vice President of Development, James Farley, Vice President for Academic Affairs, William E. Boyer, and Chaplain William W. Carpenter. From the faculty the three he appointed were Dr. Dorothy Mills, Spanish professor, Dr. John O'Neill, Political Science, and myself.

At our first meeting, the President was chairman. He continued in that role and presided over all our meetings. He was democratic, open to suggestions, encouraging participation, without dominating the discussions.

I observed the absence of any students, and the group agreed to add some. The president asked me to select them. I invited a black student, Al Boatner, major in Political Science, and Nancy Ackelson, major in Humanities. They both participated with excellent suggestions.

Dr. O'Neill represented the critical position well. He questioned if there was even a need for our considering goals. Why not just accept those formulated twenty years before and implement them?

Dean Boyer and Dr. Mills were more reticent but supported most of the suggestions. Jim Farley and Chaplain Carpenter were particularly helpful with ideas, creating a good feeling of accomplishment.

The president tried to involve everyone, and I was assigned the writing of a philosophy of the basic purpose of the college. This I submitted to the whole committee for any changes, additions or deletions.

The final statement agreed upon was, " Chapman College is a community of *learners* in the *process* of developing an environment of *free* inquiry, *creativity,* and *democratic* involvement, using the world as its campus and the accumulated intellectual, cultural, and spiritual insights of mankind as its resources. This community seeks to achieve a harmony between the intellectual and emotional life and to discover the values of *uniqueness,* life-long learning, *personal commitment* and concern for the welfare of others.''

In addition the following goals were worked out in committee meetings.

GOALS

1. To have academic excellence.
2. To encourage the learner's development toward *wholeness.*
3. To reflect the best of the *Judeo-Christian* and *other spiritual heritages.*
4. To have effective liberal arts and selected professional programs and to make them available in conventional and non-conventional ways on the various campuses of the College.
5. To have internal and external communication which results in an accurate understanding of the College.
6. To have human and financial resources to support the various College programs.

We had met in committee on Wednesday evenings at 7:00 p.m. during the school years from February 16, 1972 to June 1, 1973. It was a major achievement, and we all felt a sense of satisfaction.

I think objectives should be reviewed at least every five years as was done by President Smith in 1979. The fast changing higher education situation requires nothing less to keep abreast of the times.

Changing Our Minds

"The splitting of the atom has changed everything about war save our mode of thinking," so spoke Albert Einstein.

If mankind is to be saved from nuclear disaster and survive, the mind must be the instrument of change. Any possible survivors would envy the dead; the earth would be uninhabitable. If the *Life of Mind* is creative, then mind has an obligation to help life survive. Its own survival depends on it too. Physical force does not solve problems. It merely carries out orders from the cortex.

As President Marvin Goldberger of the California Institute of Technology says, "Quantitative differences in USA and USSR stockpiles of nuclear warheads are meaningless. If we can kill the potential opponent twice and he us six times, the idea of catchup means nothing. The USSR has 8,0000 tons of megaton bombs and USA 10,000 tons." Goldberger, who worked on the Manhattan project building the first atomic reactors, continues, "Two of our nuclear submarines (we have 40) could destroy 219 cities of 100,000 or more people in the USSR. One of their bombs on Washington could kill 300,000, destroying 60% of the hospitals with not enough blood plasma in the entire U.S. to deal with those still alive."

To think some could survive in an ecological wasteland is dinosaur mentality of which Einstein warned. Nuclear physicist Joseph Rotblatt of the University of London says, "The first strike would contaminate the atmosphere making farming impossible and mass starvation would follow." Hans Bethe, Nobel prize winning physicist who also worked on the Manhattan project, concurs. But we have the capacity beyond that extinct animal with our well-developed brain, furnishing us the reasoning and calculating ability of the left brain, and the creative and imaginitive power of the right. The anthropologist Richard Leakey estimates man's development took over 4,000,000 years. To resign ourselves to extinction is to be false to the millions of years of evolution. To align ourselves with death is to confirm the writing of Dante, "The worst place in Hell is reserved for those who were neutral in time of moral crisis." The nuclear incineration is Hell.

In 1952, on the island of Koshima, a Japanese monkey found she could wash potatoes in a stream, and they tasted better. She taught her mother, and playmates taught their mothers. By 1958 all the Koshima monkeys washed potatoes before eating them. Scientists observing this were surprised to find this habit spontaneously jumped to other islands and the mainland.

This shared awareness could add the energy among humans to achieve a nuclear free world, as they change their minds. Now the nations of the world spend one billion dollars a day on military. That could feed 50 million starving children for a year!

Psychology and Human Values

Some years ago a professor accused another member of the same department of being unscientific, because he introduced values into his teaching. I suggest this was sophomoric, because he was apparently unaware he had himself not been value free. He had valued the scientific method very highly by his criticism.

Much of the current conflict among schools of psychology is reminiscent of the professor in Charles Kingsley's *Water Babies* when he said, I discovered it and it's my bone, and if it isn't mine it isn't a bone at all!''

Methodology should differ depending on the patient in the clinic. The patient who cannot be helped by psycho-analysis (for example, some analysts don't want to deal with alcoholics) might find healing in behaviorism, and vice versa. This may be true of all schools running the gamut of therapy; each scores successes and shouldn't hesitate to refer patients to another method if unsuccessful.

And then in regard to the scientific method itself. Wouldn't it be wise for psychologists concerned with an embryonic science to keep open to the possibility of other methods of knowing? Such an authority as Maslow has inveighed against reductionism in psychological theory. For example, let's get perspective by looking at the development of another embryonic science, sociology. Lester F. Ward, the first great American Sociologist, applied principles of physics to his elementary research. His first books were *Social Statics,* and *Social Dynamics.* More recent sociologists have found this reductionism weak in studying complex human relations. Couldn't it be that complex situations in psychology, as well as sociology, need complex answers?

I remember when I was the only member of the Psychology Department in the late 30's, receiving a questionnaire from one of the measurement psychologists who shall be nameless, asking my estimate of J.B. Rhine's studies in ESP at Duke University. He collected over 300 responses from American psychologists, publishing his findings that only about 5% thought Rhine's work legitimately "scientific." Is this keeping open to new possibilities?

Abraham Maslow, in his criticism of the reductionists, seemed unaware that his theory that transcendent experiences, peak experiences, would eventually be validated by "empirical" method, and he himself might thus be reductionist. Have we completely exhausted the possibility that there may be other methods which could yield psychological facts? How about having another look at intuition?

Another reminiscence may serve as an illustration. In the 30's we used Ruch's *Introduction to Psychology* as a text for beginners in the field. He was at the University of Southern California. I had the opportunity of involving him in discussion of his rather dogmatic assertions on the I.Q. and testing. After intense questioning he finally admitted, "Well, we may not be measuring intelligence, but we are measuring something!" This was all the scientific humility I sought.

The new developments in holistic psychology give promise of a more inclusive approach, growing out of the personalistic psychology of Gordon Allport at Harvard. The philosopher, Jan Smuts, first used the term as a reaction to the "nothing but" approach of the principle of parsimony which sought to simplify metaphysical problems. Perhaps the human being is "something more than" a physical organism. Attempts to quantify all psychic phenomena may overlook significant variables.

We need a reifying of the values of life, love, liberty and dedication, as opposed to violence, hatred, addiction, and non-commitment. Psychology has a fundamental place in achieving these values for the students we work with. The setting of role models by graduate students and instructors will do much toward this achievement. Confucius said, "The greatest force in effecting social change is a living example." These values and their inversion is our next subject.

III

The Inversion of Values

When I was a college freshman listening to a lecture in Ethics, it seemed to me the two most grievous problems were *war* and *racism*. From the vantage of fifty-five years later, I am amazed that this early guess has lost none of its realism. I would today add two more to the list, *addiction* and *non-commitment*. Together they make an impressive threat to the values that matter most to me.

For each one of the four is an *inversion* of the most precious realities. Let us consider each in turn.

War and violence, its concomitant, threaten the total extinction of *life* itself, the most precious value. This has become all the more threatening since the advent of nuclear war, twenty years after my decision, reinforcing it. The classic statement of Albert Schweitzer, "Reverence for all life," is rendered meaningless in its inversion. He said, "Reverence for life is the Christian ethic of love made universal. The good preserves and promotes life; evil injures and destroys life." It is the antithesis of Jesus' teaching of the abundant life.

There are at least two factors which promote violence between individuals and war between nations. The first is polarization, which might be called the cowboy-Indian polarity. Cowboys have been magnified in America's winning of the west. They are the "good guys"; Indians, on the other hand were the "bad guys" to be subjugated, eliminated. It was a simple fervent almost religious sanction; the evil, the bad was to be stamped out, so that the good could live forever in a heaven on earth. "The only good Indian is a dead Indian" was the slogan.

Even before the western expansion, some of the colonies treated the Indians as a barbarian savage race. The exception was in Pennsylvania which offered a model in the non-violence of the Quakers. For over sixty years before the American Revolution, they made friends with the Indians. William Penn wanted a heaven on earth which included everybody. The Quakers trusted the Indians and on occasion when traveling to Philadelphia, their "city of brotherly love," left children in the company of Indian families!

This model was not followed by the other colonies who were examples of the second factor—suspicion and fear. Possibly the rigid Calvinism of the Puritans with its instilling fear and guilt encouraged this paranoia. With the lack of trust in the Indians, who responded in kind, there were killings. In contrast, no Quakers were the victims of Indian massacres during this pre-Revolutionary period. Even a savage knows when he is wished ill.

Columbus had set a pattern of violence with the Indians to the point of genocide. He said, "The natives should make good servants. They are meek with no knowledge of evil, killings, or stealing. They are without weapons." He wiped out the natives in the Antilles and took some Arawaks back to Spain. Many died or jumped overboard. On Columbus' second expedition, when the Indian chief refused to be baptized and become a Christian (because if he went to heaven he would meet Christians!), he was burned at the stake. The Queen was informed of Columbus' killings, and he was replaced as governor in disgrace.

So these factors of polarization and fear may be looked on today as possible causes of interpersonal and international misunderstanding. *Violence* and *violate* are words coming from the same root—to act unjustly, to use force without law or principle. Fear eliminates concern for others and induces the use of force.

It was Gandhi who said, "Non-violence is positive goodwill to all life. Mankind has to get out of violence, only through non-violence. Hatred can be overcome only by love.'' Einstein said of him, ''Generations to come will scarce believe that such a person ever walked upon earth,'' which of course measures our unbelief and consequent inability to effect the changes needed. It requires great courage not to hide behind a guru. Martin Luther King said, ''Non-violence is not for cowards.''

As for the psychological problem in violence, Dr. Jonas Salk, the Nobel prize winner, says, ''When you hear people defending violence, you know they are emotionally ill. Violence is an illness like cancer with no cure yet.'' I submit a knowledge of the origins is essential. There is evidence that the child learns abusive behavior in the home by the treatment of parents or older siblings. All that a child learns from being beaten is how to beat, and if no outlet is immediately available he buries his resentment to break forth months, even years, later in a more violent form.

There is disagreement whether watching violence in motion pictures or television has a catharsis effect, cleansing resentments. It has been documented that watching does teach how to administer violence. Children do learn the technique with a gun, knife, or pitchfork as varied instruments to use. The comedian, Red Skelton, made a sage remark when told that T.V. watching does not teach forms of violence. ''Why then do Kellogg's cereals and other food producers spend $150,000 for a half-minute commerical? Are they wasting their money with no children influenced to buy their product?'' Konrad Lorenz, another Nobel prize winner, says, ''I have strong doubts that watching aggressive behavior has any catharsis,'' The success of Educational T.V. cannot be disregarded.

A most significant development is the work of Dr. Paul De Boyer, a French obstetrician. Otto Rank, the psychoanalyst, had spoken of the birth trauma, that just being born has shock effect which may lead to neuroses later, even to aggressive behavior. So De Boyer evolved a method of pleasant birth with soft lights, immersion in warm water of womb temperatures, and placing the child at once on the mother's stomach instead of the separating and slapping to start breathing. The mother and baby are kept together, not as in some American hospitals where the child is placed in a glass box, separated from mother and often fed and cared for by nurses.

Dr. Willard Gaylin, psychiatrist, finds that the mother needs to cuddle the child at once or she may never feel affection for it.

A recent innovation by Dr. Konstantin Tsiolkovsky, space scientist observing the process from the area of expertise, suggests there would be less gravitational pull, less energy required to move, if the child were actually born under water thus allowing more energy to brain development. There have actually been a number of such cases in Southern California; one Jeremy Lighthouse now nearly two years old is alert, lively, with little fear and obvious high intelligence.

In an apocryphal manuscript the *Wisdom of Sirach* (200 B.C.?) are these words, "Like a eunuch who would ravish a maid is the man who would do good by violence."

Now turning from the interpersonal to the international violence of war, history is replete with its condemnation by world leaders and thinkers. The generals like Patton who said, "War is Hell, and I love every minute of it!" are criticized by philosopher Herbert Marcuse. "Obscene is not a picture of a naked person, but a fully clad general exposing his medals as rewards for killing." Immanuel Kant wrote, "A race of devils would be forced to find solutions other than war." And then there were the generals who became presidents. Washington said, "I wish as much as any man on this continent for the opportunity of turning the sword into a ploughshare." Perhaps the most trenchant indictment was the bordering on anarchy in Eisenhower's farewell address—"One of these days governments are going to have to get out of the way and let the people have peace. Every gun that is made, every warship launched, every rocket fired signifies theft from those who hunger and are not fed. We pay for one fighter plane one-half million bushels of wheat, for a bomber thirty schools, two fully equipped hospitals. We must guard against the unwarranted influence by the military-industrial complex and never let this combination endanger our liberties or democratic process." General Smedley Butler, winner of two Congressional Medals of Honor, testifying before a Congressional Committee said,

"I spent 33 years in the Marines as a muscle man for big business. I purified Nicaragua for the bankers and helped in the rape of half a dozen Central American countries for Wall Street." This quote is relevant when we see our policy in El Salvador, one of those countries, as well as in others.

The father of nuclear submarines, Admiral Rickover, retired at 83, spoke before a Senate Committee saying, "Greedy contractors with high priced lawyers evade laws, shamelessly rob the government with demands for more defense contracts on order from the Pentagon. The Secretary of Defense comes from private industry and will go back to it. They know little about defense and OK big orders as good for business and the economy. We have over 100 nuclear subs—why do we need 200? We can sink everything on the oceans now. The other side the same. Our aircraft carriers would be destroyed in the first few minutes of war." Perhaps, after our mutual destruction, new forms of life will appear on earth.

"Nuclear power should be outlawed. Radio activity is an inherent danger. For example, the new Trident II missile is a first-strike weapon, which could be triggered accidentally if computers read incoming data which is false."

Our retired military personnel know the facts about the budget and waste in the services. They no longer have anything to fear from Pentagon officials. They are beyond threats and will tell the truth.

In February 1967, Martin Luther King wrote, "If we reversed investments and gave the armed forces the anti-poverty budget, the generals could be forgiven if they walked off the battlefield in disgust. Poverty and urban problems are ignored when the guns of war become a national obsession."

The tragedy in all this is that it brings both sides closer to war than farther away from it.

Perhaps the poet Thomas Hardy's pessimism is on the mark even today—

"Peace on earth the angels sing it.
We pay a million priests to bring it,
After 2000 years of Mass,
We've gotten as far as poison gas."

The world is spending 500 billion on nonproductive armaments which make it less not more secure. There is enough nerve gas stored in the US to destroy over a trillion human beings, many times the world population. Louis Fieser, the inventor of napalm used in Vietnam when questioned about his conscience said, "It's not my business to deal with moral questions."

The neutron bomb now can destroy people without harming property, leaving it intact, for whom? A few survivors? The Royal Swedish Academy of Science after a two year study by 22 American, Soviet, and European scientists publishes that 750 million people would be killed outright, plus 340 million injured in a nuclear war using less than *half* of the weapons in present stockpiles of the US and USSR (1982).

Our government's thirst to keep amassing stockpiles seem irrational to the point of paranoia. One Poseidon nuclear submarine can destroy the 100 largest cities in the USSR yet we have an estimated 50 of them. The Pentagon has 1500 lobbyists in Washington.

The government has tried to get the Environmental Protection Agency to permit the sinking in the ocean of "obsolete" nuclear submarines!

Two ounces of plutonium inhaled in equal doses could give cancer to 4 billion people. Yet the world produced four tons in 1970 and 18 tons in 1975! The cruise missile we are planning can make a first strike possible, because it eliminates tracking and thus a nuclear stalemate. On order now are 20,000 missiles of the ordinary variety at 42 million dollars each (January 1982).

Freud would have a comment on this preoccupation of man with missiles as phallic symbols and their feeling of impotence.

This stockpiling of bombs and chemicals is justified, the authorities say, because the Communists are not to be trusted. Yet we signed the Geneva Convention Articles which we broke three times in Vietnam by (1) saturation bombing, (2) mass moving of populations, and (3) genocide. Are we to be trusted? We are the only nation to use the atomic bomb on population, not on military centers. Our leaders talk of a traditional type war with the USSR in Europe, but does anyone believe that if either side began to lose, it would not employ any means including nuclear to win? These leaders would not be threatened because our nuclear hideaway in the Blue Ridge Mountains, which was 20 years in the building, would have air, food, and water with a staff of 1000. It costs $42 million a year for upkeep. But certainly the Russians know about this and are capable of blasting it. As for the general population, the accepted studies indicate 200 million in the U.S. would die in the first attack. The others suffering from radiation burns would have little means of survival and would envy the dead. There is no civil defense possible, and rehearsals are merely playing games to reassure the public. In a Harvard study of doctor and hospital facilities, 80% of all doctors would be dead with most hospitals destroyed.

These facts lead to the consideration of ethics and war. President Kennedy said, "Wars will exist until the day when the conscientious objector enjoys the same prestige as the warrior." Curiously, Henry Kissinger when Secretary of State wrote, "Conscientious objection must be reserved for only the great moral issues, and Vietnam isn't of that magnitude." While he was posturing, Captain Michael Heck, winner of the Distinguished Flying Cross, became a conscientious objector saying, "War creates evil far greater than anything it may try to prevent. I no longer can participate even in loading bombs or refueling."

The American historian Henry Steele Commager wrote, "Conscientious objection rooted in moral faith is essential for the health of any nation." And General Omar Bradley said, "The world has achieved power without conscience, we know the mystery of the atom while rejecting the Sermon on the Mount."

There is something sacriligious about the Navy naming a new nuclear submarine, "Corpus Christi" (Body of Christ). Mitchell Snyder fasted for two months until the name was changed. He said, "Once you call a nuclear sub "God," you strip away the last barrier to its use."

Even a church seeking to practice the Sermon by a gesture of goodwill to a wartorn country seems to make the government feel threatened. The Mennonite Central Committee before Christmas, 1981, tried to send notebooks and pencils to Cambodian children, who had been impoverished and frightened by our military adventure. The American government refused to grant this act of sympathy.

Roger Rosenblatt, correspondent for *Time* magazine, traveled to five wartorn areas to find out the reaction of children to their terrifying experience of seeing parents killed, and being powerless to help them. In Northern Ireland a 14 year old boy said, "No, I don't want revenge. It's not right to kill anyone." In Israel a 10 year old boy said, "What good is all this revenge! I would like to live in a world without soldiers."

In Cambodia a 10 year old boy defined, "Revenge means I would try to make my enemies into better people." And a 15 year old Vietnamese boy who saw others killed for food said, "I would not kill in order to live."

Rosenblatt interviewed 60 children finding they were forgiving after suffering abuse and torture! He writes, "I felt like a fool for the type of civilization we have foisted on them."

The Junior R.O.T.C. in the public schools according to one boy teaches, "When you kill the first man you are a little queasy, but after that you do it for duty and honor." College R.O.T.C.'s pay $100 a month and give 90% of the class "A" grades, yet have 90% dropouts!

The scientists must take a stand on conscience. "Science no longer has time to work out problems of overpopulation and ecological crisis. The major task is the elimination of war," writes Konrad Lorenz. The noted anthropologist, Ashley Montague, summarizes this section on life and its antithesis— Violence and War, "The most unnatural and artificial of all human activities is war."

The overarching supreme problem of our day is survival of the human race. There will be no need to work on other problems without peace.

The second problem we listed was racism, race prejudice and hatred. Seneca, the Roman philosopher said, "Hate drinks half its own poison." Too often the hater thinks his potion will do away with the object of his antipathy, but the only way to eliminate an enemy is to make a friend of him. The two greatest spiritual leaders of all time attest to this. Jesus said, "Love your enemies," and Buddha taught, "Hatred does not cease by hatred, but by love." The concept of love requires some contemplation. The Greeks, who had a word for everything, realized there were forms of love requiring shades of meaning. So they used three different words, *eros, phileo* and *agape.* Our contemporary idea is largely the erotic type. Motion pictures, television and romance magazines emphasize sexual love. Anders Nygren, the theologian, wrote *Eros and Agape,* in which he compared the two, but he does not feel *agape* depends on *eros. Agape* is difficult to comprehend for the erotic type. *Eros* is concerned with getting love—*agape* with giving, yes, even sacrificial giving. The mother who sacrifices for her child is an example. It is a word rarely used in Greek except in translating the New Testament. However, the distinction is valid and instructive for those who see love as mainly physical.

Phileo is commonly used in its Greek meaning "love of friends." William Penn's naming of Philadelphia means the city of "brotherly love."

The relation of *love* to *life* is evident. It was the Chinese sage Laotzu who observed, "Love is victorious in attack and sure in defense. Heaven arms with love those it would not see destroyed." But we do not believe in the value of love. Another Chinese philosopher, Mengtzu, lamented, "Love conquers hate as water conquers fire. Men's deeds of love today are like throwing a cup of water on a burning cartload of wood. Then they say, 'See, water does not conquer fire,' and they become less loving."

This disbelief is well stated by Confucius who hearing Laotzu teach, "Recompense injury with kindness," remonstrated, "Nonsense, recompense kindness with kindness and injury with justice." A remarkable example of this is the extreme motion picture *Birth of a Nation* in 1915. Its indictment of war also preached race prejudice!

Did Laotzu win the argument by answering, "If you recompense injury with kindness, all have the chance to become kind by your example''? Laotzu is interested in bringing about change in the one who injures another, while Confucius feels he will only take advantage of the love shown. Laotzu believes man can be redeemed, but not so Confucius. They have different views of human nature. Jesus believed in redeeming love.

Aristophanes after the Peloponnesian War prayed, "Mingle again the kindred of the nations in the alchemy of love and with a finer essence of forgiveness temper our minds.'' Our concept of international law is not based on love but on justice. Plato wrote *The Republic* trying to define justice. He concluded it meant *balance* between the classes, rulers, soldiers, and workers. This he developed from the analogy of a human being whose body, mind, and spirit functioned in harmony. But this justice assumed there was a lower slave class! How about justice for those people? Apparently Plato himself was not satisfied with the Republic because he wrote two more books, *The Statesman* and *The Laws,* trying to justify a basic fallacy, as if he had some pangs of conscience.

Martin Luther King who wrote his doctorate on Plato saw this, for he wrote, "If we keep repeating the idea of justice as an eye for an eye, we will soon all be blind.'' The upper class is involved in the vicissitudes of the lower class, and in the treatment of it must share the responsibility for its acts. In his Baccalaureate address to Chapman graduates in 1928, Dr. Theodore Soares, professor at the California Instititute of Technology, told them, "The man who steals a loaf of bread to feed a starving family is a criminal in our society, while the man who steals a million dollars in business deals becomes a captain of industry.'' Justice is not blind in our civilization. Nils Bohr, the physicist Nobel Prize winner, wrote, "One cannot know another human being in the light of love and justice at the same time.'' We must choose which attitude toward other humans is the basis for our actions. As we judge, so shall we be judged.

All of the great religions have been concerned with overcoming man's egocentricity. "They may appear different but beneath the surface they try to overcome egocentricity by the same method—love," writes Arnold Toynbee, the historian. Bertrand Russell, the philosopher, adds, "What the world needs is Christian love and compassion." (Buddha taught compassion for all creatures.) Martin Luther King combined the two problems of war and prejudice when he said, "I cannot separate the problem of racism from my concern about the war in Vietnam."

In our early history President John Quincy Adams wrote, "The ills of war and slavery are man-made and man should abolish both," and Lord Caradon speaking as British Ambassador to the United Nations said, "The problem of race is inextricably bound up with the problem of war."

Our interdependence might be illustrated thus: Suppose you boarded an airplane and discovered next to you a person of a different race or a known Communist or criminal sought by the authorities—what would you do? You wish him a safe journey, of course. Why? You are on the same plane. Just so, we are all travelers on space-earth and had better not destroy it.

Now we turn to the problem of *addiction*, the inversion of *liberty* as a value. It is related to prejudice in that it denies liberty, but rather the freedom of the self than the one who is the object of prejudice. Self-destruction is becoming epidemic among youth. The second greatest cause of death among college students is suicide. What percent of them are drug or alcohol induced we do not know. By some perverse reasoning many think its use will bring them more freedom. Usage continued causes *abulia,* a disease of the will, in which they are unable to distinguish between goals and sink inactive doing nothing purposeful. William James who experimented briefly with drugs wrote, "The reshaping of our inner attitudes leads to the reshaping of our outward circumstances." We need to be free from destructive attitudes as much as from prejudice. *Freedom means the opportunity to take advantage of the unexpected.* Addiction renders us impotent.

The last problem, which is also a current one, is *non-commitment.* It is the inversion of the value of *loyalty.* It is related to the other problem. Non-commitment means no goals, no motivation, just as for the addict. Josiah Royce, the

American philosopher, wrote a book called *The Philosophy of Loyalty*. To lose the self in something greater is to find genuine happiness. The person who is self-seeking is never satisfied. The greater the cause, the more inclusive, the better. We come full circle with the example we used of Schweitzer at the outset. He had reverence for *all* life, not just the human species. Today, more than ever, we need loyalty to all life and beyond nature to the planet itself. Our problem is—we need to start with the primary group, the family. Experiments in living with a chosen group, sexual interrelations among several couples whose children are regarded as "belonging to all" with adults as parents are interesting. It remains for time to tell what sort of adults the children become. From the family to the neighborhood and then to the larger community, state, and nation and now the United Nations the way seems clear. Josiah Royce called the "beloved community" another name for the Kingdom of God on earth.

Selecting a larger purpose on principle means uniting with all persons of goodwill to accomplish mutually chosen goals. Many people do not feel important as individuals in having any effect on their community or government at the national level. It was Confucius who said, "The greatest force in effecting change is a living example," and Norman Cousins wrote, "There is great power in personal advocacy of a principle."

We have a duty in a negative fashion as well, to be subversive to racism, war, and economic injustice. William James in his famous lecture at Stanford University called for a "moral equivalent of war" by using this power against the enemies of mankind—human suffering, starvation, poverty, and war instead of fighting each other. Centuries before, Erasmus, the great humanist wrote, "Christians should not fight except in the noblest of battles against love of money, anger and fear. Man is born for friendship, mutual aid, love, laughter for healing and tears for pity."

So we have outlined the values past and present—life, love, liberty, and loyalty. The accent affirmative hopefully will come and their inversion in a sick society will disappear. Sophocles says in *Antigone,* "Evil at times will be thought to be good."

In Lane Seminary, in Cincinnati, 1834, a group of students debated nights on slavery. They concluded it was wrong. Accordingly they invited free negroes to their classes on the basis of social equality. The faculty and administration decided this endangered endowment and "men surrender some individual rights on entering the college. Free inquiry must be subordinate to the interests of continuing the institution and faculty should be the jude of this. Social public actions distract from studies, excite the community and bear on national issues." (Note that study should not bear on national issues.) The students responded that the faculty had no power to regulate student action prior to actual abuse (which sounds like correct legal procedure). They continued, "The object of education is ascertaining truth and how to act. We are bound to do whatever truth dictates"—a noble statement. They withdrew and with some of the faculty helped start Oberlin College.

Beyond Criticism

How can we enrich our environment? How can we be creative? We must be creative in our suggestions about creativity.

The critic is destroyed with his own criticism. How does this happen? First, all who hear the critic may judge him by his judgment. Jesus phrased it, "Judge not, that ye be not judged, for as you judge so you will be judged." People know what sort of person we are by our statements. Again, Jesus said, "Blessed are the pure in heart! They shall see God." Those who bear malice are blind to the good in others; the pure in heart see good in all and everywhere!

We learn a second principle at this point from psychology. The man who criticizes a fault in another is too aware of the same fault in himself, and he uses a "projection mechanism." He projects his fault into another to hide his own, and paradoxically he is revealed by it. It is the possession of a characteristic which enables us to identify the same characteristic in others.

Real intelligence has a sentimental quality; it is insight, that is, it not only sees the fault, it *understands* it. Empathy is the quality of putting ourselves in place of either the victim or wrongdoer.

The Life of Mind

The salvation of the mind lies in the suggestion that the critical tendency is only a stage in development of history. The college student who feels he must criticize everything and everybody eventually graduates. He really graduates when he can deal with faults not just by criticism, but by *identifying himself with them.* Some never reach this maturity. Those who do, create a Phoenix out of the ashes.

If it is true that man now seeks food in a starving environment, if he is poisoning himself and knows it not, there are two things to be done. First, a warning must be sounded. Poison must be labeled for what it is—wrong thinking, wrong acting, wrong control, ugliness and worship of false gods. If the diagnosis is correct then we are ready for the prognosis.

Criticism is negative evaluation. Appreciation is positive evaluation. Criticism is an attitude of mind which is governed by the fear of being excelled. It is mind subject to an emotion and therefore no mind at its best. Mind is the nearest to divine in the human. It is the instrument of our salvation. Conscience is the mind plus consideration of others, an ethical addition.

Appreciation is looking at others and things with an affirmative accent. It sees the good in the true and understands. It thus encourages the other person to be better and truer. It is mind at its best without fear of losing status as a handicap. It sees some instance of good in a stranger or even an enemy and thus gives God a chance to effect a reconciliation. As the Japanese Haiku poet says,

> In the city park
> Contemplating cherry trees
> Strangers are like friends.

The creative mind produces ideas. They are to it what blossoms are to a flowering plant, or fruit to a tree. The discovery of science is just as much a product of the creative mind as is the masterpiece of art or literature.

Jung gives another example: "All the important problems of life are fundamentally insoluble, but living means growth through them and beyond toward the spirit." As the mind is more creative it sees more alternatives to problems which confront the person, and as it selects an alternative it grows even more possibilities. As we select the right way through a maze, we are led out into richer and more productive solutions. Jung continues, "The new way demands to be discovered. It is like something of the psyche that is alive."

Centuries ago, Sir Thomas Brown spoke of this creative potential, "There is something in us that can be without us, though it hath no history of what it was before, nor can it tell how it entered us."

The test of this creative mind is "not what men do when they know what to do, but how they act when they don't know," as Chaplain William Coffin of Yale puts it. Examples of the phenomenon are embodied in our revolutionary war leaders, whom Adlai Stevenson called, "the most soundly educated group of radicals the world has known. The balance between vision and practicality reflects the wisdom of well-nourished minds."

Whitehead defined peace as, "the intuition of firmaments."

Today the United Nations argues the need of world economy, that the suffering of the third world countries is inevitably our suffering as well, that mercy is the way to survival of all. Curiously, those who speak of survival of the fittest forget that Darwin himself said, "In numberless animal societies the struggle between individuals for the means of existence disappears and is replaced by cooperation."

So the creative mind is fulfilled in a creative community working toward creative peace. To paraphrase Plato, "It matters not if the ideal |world| has ever been or ever will be, for he who has imagined it will live in the manner of that |world|." If we could imagine ourselves out in space perhaps on another planet, we might see Earth with Archibald McLeish as , "small

and blue and beautiful in the eternal silence where it floats
and see ourselves as riders on the earth together.''

Now let us consider the origins of creativity in brain functions.

IV

The Origins of Creativity

Dr. Roger Sperry of the California Institute of Technology discovered the functions of the left and right brain in experiments in the 60's. The left brain specializes in language functions, reasoning, logic, and analysis. The two halves work together through the corpus callosum. One half can "teach" the other half. The right brain specializes in the imagination, intuition, and synthesis. Sperry was awarded the Nobel prize in medicine for this research.

Schools traditionally have accented the reasoning, the logical, and the analytical. Truth about reality was discovered by ratiocination, a discursive route like a maze. But truth may find reality by a direct flash of inspiration. The two may complement each other as in Einstein's scientific discoveries. Recent studies at M.I.T. of creative scientists confirm this. Note it is true of scientists particularly. Bertrand Russell said, "It must emerge as a sudden imaginative insight." In 1979 Dr. Betty Edwards, using Sperry's work as basic, wrote the book, *Drawing on the Right Side of the Brain*. The left hand is controlled by the right brain, using the left hand as the dreamer, the creator, in painting and drawing. She finds that artists express wonder and excitement, in an almost mystical state of mind. They are alert, relaxed, and free in expressing ideas. They perceive life as more than words and numbers.

These findings have significance for psychology of religion also. Most authorities on mysticism, for example, spoke of it as beyond the intellect, but ineffable, with no focus in the physical structure. Now we find its place not beyond the intellect, but a part of it. Our task in education then is "to relocate the role of words as a complement to non-verbal signs and celebrations," according to the artist Sister Corita. She will paint words into her drawings thus attempting to combine the two. This is a good example of the manner in which the logical and intuitive areas of the brain can work together.

In the creative act, the person adds something to the existential world which did not exist before. Does this mean to break the law of conservation of energy? Or was this essence in the potential the real meaning? Perhaps this essential meaning is that which is immortal. Van Hartmann in his aesthetic theory spoke of objective immortality, that is, we are immortal in our works, our art. This is another possibility.

Carl Jung wrote, "The creative act will forever elude human understanding." He is anti-rational on creativity, holding that archetypes underlie all creativity, accounting for its universal appeal (music, for example, is enjoyed by all cultures).

So the psychologists bring us ultimately to philosophy. Jung sounds much like Plato. Intellectualism puts man at the mercy of the instinctive unconscious. Dreams bring back the *recollection* of the primitive as a catharsis. In the *Meno* Plato held that all knowledge was recollection. The task of the teacher (Socrates) is to stimulate this birth as a "midwife of ideas." See **An Example of Creativity**, page 72. Einstein said, "Imagination is more important than knowledge." In modern philosophy, Reichenbach, a friend of Einstein, pointed out, "The critical attitude may make man incapable of discovery," while Croce identified aesthetics as the way of knowing beauty, and logic as the way of knowing truth. It was left for the poet to unify them. "Beauty is truth, truth beauty," wrote Keats.

Perhaps, if we emphasize the total function using logic and imagination, we won't be repeating old and failing methods for solving social, political and international issues. New alternatives would be revealed by the heretofore unused areas.

More creative approaches of persuasion and non-violence would find answers. It was Camus who said, "Great ideas come into the world as gently as doves. If we listen, we shall hear amid the uproar of nations, a flutter of wings, a gentle stirring of hope."

Perhaps the mind is a womb of ideas. It is impregnated by imagination. The embryonic conception is shaped by reason during the gestation period. The longer the gestation period, the better the idea. Linus Pauling was asked where he got so many ideas. "I make them up and then I think about them, discarding the bad ones."

A good idea is one that survives the birth trauma. So the mind may be a tomb of ideas, as well as the womb. Ideas may be stillborn. Education must eliminate any straitjacket, formal static curricula, and give the life of mind a chance. The creation of new ideas is preferable to being a mirror of supposed absolute truth.

There are some scientists who regard mind as existing apart from the organic brain. We have already mentioned Roger Sperry. Dr. Wilder Penfield, the Canadian neuro-surgeon, and Karl Pribram of Stanford University are others. Pribram's experiments find a placebo effect in blocking pain by generating creative endorphins in the brain. The existence of endorphins seems reminiscent of Plotinus' theory of emanations. Dr. Jampolsky, at the Center for Attitudinal Healing, uses Primbram's discoveries. For example, a patient may *visualize* cancer as a castle being attacked, overcome, and destroyed by their "healing germs." Dr. Silvio Varon of University of California San Diego and Dr. Carl Cotman of University of California Irvine find that the brain produces chemicals to repair itself after injury by using connective tissue with transplants. This creative discovery should lead to remarkable advancements in brain functions.

Sperry writes that consciousness is an "emergent of brains," the nature of which cannot be predicted by the brain's elements. Penfield wrote in *The Mystery of Mind* (1975), "There is no good evidence that the brain alone can carry out the work the mind does." Penfield speaks of a "creative flash forming new entities."

It may be that there is evidence of actual physical creativity by the brain in releasing endorphins. This could account for success in stress situations of almost superhuman feats of strength, and Indian mystics seeming to be oblivious to pain when needles are pressed through the skin. Other examples are reduced pain in dental extractions and the "natural" childbirth (LaMaze). The triggering of endorphins may release adrenalin.

The perceptive right half of the brain, the imaginative, the visualizing, the intuitive, is the dreamer, the creator in science or out. It may be that which actually characterizes the person, that makes him unique, distinguishing him.

Attempts have been made to accelerate the ability by the use of drugs. I remember meeting Aldous Huxley when he was experimenting with the use of peyote, a berry used in Indian religious ceremonies. He tells of it in *The Doors of Perception*. Gerald Heard, his friend, lecturer on Science for B.B.C., used LSD. His student, William Forthman (now a professor of philosophy at California State University Northridge) told me in 1946 of his euphoria in its use—"Paul, the sounds of music were the opening of heaven, the colors I saw were vibrating, the most beauty I ever experienced." Later (1962) Carlos Casteneda wrote of the imaginary visions in *Teaching of Don Juan-Yaqui Way of Knowing* and *Journey to Ixtlan*, which won him a Ph.D. at the prestigious U.C.L.A. in Anthropology.

I have one caveat about the use of drugs as aids. They indicate an impatience, a desire for instant euphoria. There are examples in the history of religion showing the same results through meditation. St. Theresa, her disciple, St. John of the Cross, and St. Catherine tell of visualizations. Loyola writes of contemplating a stick of wood until it vibrates, coming alive as he becomes a part of the imagined history of the wood back to the tree from which it came. He advocates contemplating the birth of Jesus, the night, the stars, the shed, the animals, the shepherds, the wisemen, the baby, Mary and Joseph, until they become alive, as he is actually present. Events in the life of Jesus are similarly visualized (*i.e.* the Crucifixion) until one *understands* his character.

The way of meditation without the accompanying stimulation is a greater tribute to the capacity, the genius of the creative mind. Creativity cannot be forced. We can set up the stage when some problem disturbs our thoughts then relax and let the solution, be it in art or science, happen. Great artists have self confidence that they will be, as the poet Witter Byner says, "Content though it goes, that it came"!

At the other extreme is the deadening effect of television which does all the visualizing for the individual. Reading was a help because he had to imagine what the action or scene described might be. Television dulls the imagination, making the watcher only an observer, seldom a participant creator. But the creative is now working on T.V. By using synthesizers of musical sounds, together with fleeting formless images resonating and fascinating the auditing observer, some visual perceptions change by use of laser beams enveloping the observer. These are called *holograms,* an interesting development combining art and science. Radio gave the listener a chance to create a picture of what he heard.

Children graduate with no ability in creative thinking. We should teach curiosity not conformity, dissentient not consentient thinking, problem solving, and, when a plateau period brings worry and defeatism, have them turn to something else and in relaxing, the idea comes. As children begin, all are creative. By brainstorming, originality—risk taking problems challenge the imagination in a unique way, not the same as usually taught by conformity. Brainstorming may start with all sorts of ideas, some far out, foolish, eccentric, but several may open the way to a sound one. Life presents us with new situations needing solving—a high IQ won't necessarily be best at it. Remain a child perpetually. It gives zest to life.

All of which could be applied not only to children's problems but the world problems of USSR-USA with both sides now hardening their positions and increasing military expenditures. Admiral Gene R. LaRocque warns, "Never in history has there been a buildup in armaments not resulting in a war." Apparently the solution is not piling up more death dealing weapons than the other side, but both sides participating in problem solving. They should explore the interests of each and create attractive solutions for mutual satisfaction of them. This creating enterprise could actually be a form of competition for the best answers, thus satisfying some of the traditional adversary positions without going to that extreme.

As we found in children's problem solving, brainstorming for solutions should be an ongoing process without stopping to make judgments which tends to stop creativity. Too, there may be complex or many answers not just one.

Consulting experts in the field of USSR-USA relations helps if those nations haven't already arrived at a hard position. Knowledge of each country and each ideology helps along with their belief and value systems. To show this knowledge brings respect at least from the opponent. Even further showing awareness of some of the problems the other side may have and some sympathy in solving them can break a stalemate. There are always mutually shared interests in any situation. The problem is to find them and negotiate their achievement.

The short paragraphs we turn to now penetrate particular areas like *imagination, intelligence, interpretation, action,* and an example of creative *recollection.*

Imagination and Truth
The story is told of the little boy who drew a picture and said it was a steam engine. "It's not like what it is; it's like it seems," he explained. How true is imaginary life? The man suffering from D.T.'s sees pink elephants, yet we deny their existence. The psychologist experimenting with peyote or LSD finds the commonplace objects alive with beauty and wonder. Somewhere we make our peace with the facts in our imagination.

When life becomes too boring with the humdrum reality of things, then we flee to imagination, intoxication, or art.

Is beauty true? We are fascinated by a certain person's beauty and "gild of lily." The sense of perfection leads us to heights of praise and joy. The sense is within us, not in the object. This symmetry, balance, comes from within. We are born with it. It is Kant's categories; it is the gestalt. It puts all things in proportion and in perspective. Plato was right: the idea is eternal.

The creator changes the objects of his perception. Thus he lives more happily than the critic. The critic takes life as he finds it. He doesn't like it but does little more than express his dislike. Thus he is usually pessimistic and cynical. He has little hope and less faith.

The creator sees alternatives. There seem many ways opening as if by magic, as he works out the creation. The more he creates, the more ways of developing he begins to see.

As he sees these, he modifies his creation and thus it begins to take the shape of his own individuality. It becomes uniquely his. Thus, when we observe paintings, we speak of the style of Van Gogh, for example, and we also see the imitator.

Aristotle spoke of arts as the imitation of nature, but it is more than that, unless we regard the artist himself as a part of nature. This imitator has the quality of appreciation but may lack creative ability.

Dead End

The more intelligent we are the more alternatives we see in any situation. But even more, foresight can look ahead in each of these and see probable chances of success or failure in each. We don't want to choose a dead end.

It's like trails opening before us in the mountains. A friend tells of his experience in a mountain camp where the campers hiked out to a point for evening vespers. After the service he straggled behind the group and took a wrong trail. It was dark, and he decided to lie down in the trail and sleep till daylight. In the morning he started down a trail and had gone a short ways when he was confronted by a bear coming up the trail. It was not only a dead end but a danger. He turned and went up and the bear did not follow him. He found the right trail and returned to camp.

There is the further point to be made, that choosing the right trail gives us confidence for the future judging of alternatives which we might encounter.

The Urgency of the Moment

The more we regard ourselves as an instrument in the hand of the creator, the more we are conscious of the factor of chance contacts with persons and situations. As I meet and talk with a particular person, I must always keep in the periphery of my consciousness the opportunity of saying the encouraging thing. On the other hand, if I am cynical or skeptical and have no faith in the universe of which I am part, I merely negate my own existence and make it meaningless. I pass this way but once, and I have the God-given chance to make each moment count. This does not blind me to the problems of the world but allows me to do something about them.

Interpretation and Creation

Critics have said that modern America does not appreciate creation and creator, but only interpretation and interpreter. Let us examine this assertion. It seems true that we do glorify the musicians and conductors, the Pinzas and Toscaninis, and not the composers. We seem to understand the actors and applaud them rather than the playwrights. Shakespeare gives Hamlet the words, "The play is the thing, in which I'll catch the conscience of the king."

We build vast edifices to hear symphonies and present great drama and house masterpieces of art. But our scholarships go to those who study to interpret, not to the struggling composers and budding artists.

Perhaps we are too young a civilization to be called a culture. May it not be that interpretation is a form of creation? Our understanding reaches its limits with interpretation. It is not ready for creation or the creator. It is learning to appreciate, and learning comes through repetition. When we hear a classic repeated many times, we begin to understand. But the composition by the young creative composer, which we hear for the first time, seems full of dissonance because it is not like that to which we have grown accustomed.

The world did not need Beethoven's *Fifth Symphony* until he composed it. Now that we have heard it, we would be impoverished without it!

Productive Action

Production without possession
Action without assertion—

Laotzu

One of the classic examples of dissentient thinking is found in Laotzu. Western civilization particularly in America has the generally accepted goal of action and production. It is accepted, without thinking, that production is possible without action, yes, aggressive action.

But what if we consider the alternative result as a goal? Could our pragmatic assumption stand the idea of producing without personal gain or self adulation? Is it contradictory to think in such terms?

Perhaps if we accept the alternative, we could again find ourselves creative beyond our highest imagination. There would be no strings attached, no talk of "how much will it cost and what will it pay?"

The question will rather be, does it lift the human spirit, does it inspire the soul? And what about action without assertion? If possession and the headlong race to "get ahead," which means ahead of others regardless, is suspect, surely not assertion! With all of the classes being offered in assertion training, to some extent resulting from the sexist attitude toward women, the need for assertion should be apparent.

But should this need be carried to all members of the community? Persons who are always assertive, demanding their rights in every circumstance, become obnoxious after their constant harangue. Was it not true that women were reacting to this continual assertiveness on the part of men?

Assertive persons are constantly confronting someone about

something. Perhaps the key is to examine what the confrontation is about. If it is as trivial as a husband's assertion to his wife's dress, or on the other hand, her comment on his selection of ties, why be assertive?

Assertion should be reserved for times of violation of the person as a human being and other worthy causes. Always insisting on one's rights raises the question of one's own responsibilities as well.

So, perhaps wisely, it may be suggested that our actions need not always involve carrying a chip on one's shoulder, being too assertive. While it is right as a defense against mistreatment, it may be suspect in always seeking social status. A better word with less confrontation signified might be *affirming* instead of asserting. It has less ego, less possibility of challenging by force, as an opponent!

An Example of Creativity
The genius of Plato is well illustrated in the *Meno*, a Socratic dialog. The work is beautifully crafted so that it becomes a form which can be diagramed. There are three characters representing three reactions to Socrates, the central figure; Anytos, a general and political leader; Meno, a rich young man with his slave (notice with no name). They are discussing whether virtue can be taught.

Each in turn is engaged in conversation, and Socrates attempts to find the truth by inquiry. Knowing Meno's aristocratic and superior attitude, he compliments him on his brains as a native of Thessaly, while there is "a famine of brains" in Athens. Meno is caught off guard, giving simple obvious answers to Socrates who pursues relentlessly (the gadfly of Athens urging men to think and know why they should or shouldn't follow a particular course of action). Among other major points which Socrates makes is that truth is not necessarily determined by winning an argument. This is profound in its implication that perhaps our system of debating is flawed. In college debates the emphasis is on winning not necessarily finding the truth, which may be incidental. Perhaps this is true even of Congress!

Meno concludes after much questioning that Socrates is like a stingray that numbs everyone it touches as well as itself. Socrates admits he doesn't know but insists that man must try to find out; that by consulting his soul, he will remember. This amazing view that every man has available this source of knowledge from birth, because he is immortal, is the faith of Socrates vouchsafed by Plato.

This is too much for Meno who believes he can purchase knowledge from the Sophists (who know or pretend they know) and thus avoid the strenuous task of thinking.

To show Meno what is missing, Socrates turns to Meno's slave boy. By dint of simple questions the boy is led to work out of the Pythagorean theorem. Socrates thus shows Meno that knowledge is available to the supposedly inferior, and thus from Meno's point of view, ignorant.

I believe this to be the beginning of true democracy, not just democracy for the wealthy. John Dewey saw this in America as a philosopher of education, when he taught that democracy can only survive with an educated electorate. Not just voting, but knowing the issues is basic.

The third participant, Anytos, enters. He is anti-intellectual, suspicious of the Sophists ("madmen" he calls them) as corrupters of youth. (This was a charge he later made at a trial of Socrates as one of his accusers). When Socrates asks what his experience has been with them, Anytos asserts he has nothing to do with any. Anytos is an example of what happens when we don't have direct contact with people, and our own fears conjure up all sorts of false notions.

He recommends "well bred gentlemen of Athens" rather than Sophists for teachers. He leaves, angrily warning Socrates to be careful with his talk. Socrates shows no resentment, forgiving Anytos because Anytos doesn't know any better.

We might attempt creating a diagram showing the possible degree of success Socrates had in each instance.

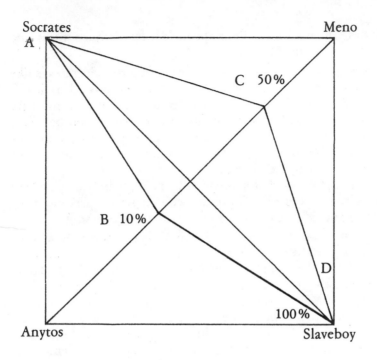

The darker line indicates this degree showing 10% toward Anytos, 50% toward Meno and 100% toward the boy. These are arbitrary evaluations but serve the purpose which shows the unbalanced result with the imperfect figure ABCD compared to a perfect square. This creation may have added value in showing Plato's concern for balance and harmony. Even the master of dialog, Socrates, did not achieve it.

Truth is found in dialog. This is the major teaching. If any refuse to be part of it, to that extent truth is not complete. This is the tragedy of those who are fearful, bearing ill will toward the whole process that could be their enlightenment. Truth is thus born deformed and all suffer. In this life we see through a "glass darkly." In a democracy all must participate not only to bring it strength but so all possible points of view are considered forming a more reasoned, more truthful decision.

The Character of Socrates

While the *Meno* records the master at work, other dialogs attest to Socrates' greatness as a person. In the *Phaedrus* he warns us, "No written discourse deserves to be treated seriously. The best of them only remind us of what we already know." They cannot reply when you ask a question; therefore the written work becomes authoritarian.

He continues in the *Euthydemas*, "Do not mind whether teachers are good or bad, but think only of the love of wisdom. Examine her truly. If she be evil turn away, but if she is what I believe her to be, then follow her and be of good cheer." Thus he points beyond the written page and beyond the human, including himself, toward the ideal of wisdom.

He repeats this in *Republic*. "The real lover of wisdom must reach after all truth with all his might."

A passage in the *Symposium* reminds one of Paul's I Corinthians Chapter 13. Could Paul have read this and been inspired by it centuries later?

In *The Symposium,* which is my favorite of all the dialogs, we read this tribute to Love—"Love wrongs neither God nor man and is wronged by none. Nothing happens to love by violence, nothing love does is violent. Love is just, full of temperance. No pleasure is stonger than love. Love is greater than all others in courage. Love makes peace among men, provides gentleness and banishes savagery, gives goodwill, hates to give illwill, is a pilot, a savior. Love is so wise a poet that he makes everybody poets, even those who before had no music in their souls. By contemplating beautiful things in due order, suddenly the person will behold beauty marvelous, the eternal Beauty itself which lends beauty to all things in part which are in part ugly." The *Symposium* is Plato at his creative best. No wonder Whitehead says, "All the history of Western philosophy is a series of footnotes to Plato."

The trial and imprisionment of Socrates is portrayed by Plato so graphically we actually feel present at the time and place. The *Apology* quotes Socrates before the judges, "Something divine and spiritual has been with me since boyhood, a voice—When my sons grow up if they care more for money than goodness, reproach them.—No evil can befall a good man in life or death and God does not neglect him." Later in prison he says to Crito, "We must not do wrong in return for evil to anyone however we may be treated by him. It is never right to do any injustice or return injustice when one is evily treated."

Finding Beauty in Creating It

Socrates prayed for beauty in the inner man. He was aware of his own physical ugliness, knowing nothing could be done to change it. But he had faith that spiritual growth was possible.

What is it in the human that responds to the beauty of the universe? Why does man stare at the glow of the setting sun? What is the magnet in a field of flowers waving in the morning breeze? What chord in us responds to a musical rhapsody?

Whatever it may be, it satisfies us that this universe is our home. We are not strangers here.

There is not only the awe and wonder of the universe, but the joy and love of human nature. We are not alone. There are others who share our response to the universe and in the sharing find this beauty in the inner man. God answers prayer by making us open our eyes to become aware of physical beauty, but also to penetrate with the spiritual eye the heart of another person.

Life can become rich and significant as we develop this innate beauty in response to the beauty of nature and human nature. Socrates had the beauty he prayed for as he found it in a dialogue with others.

A young art student said he was unaware of certain shadings of color until he had tried to create a picture.

This seed of beauty is in all of us. All it needs is cultivating through the creative urge.

When the world of everyday blocks us at every turn, when every act of attempted adjustment is frustrated, when every gesture of friendly help is rebuffed, then we appreciate that perfect thrill of creation, the world of imagination clothes in wonder every glance we take. Out of the dim unknown comes a mystic figure who encourages, who inspires, who satisfies. There must be immortality, or reincarnation, if you wish, when this perfect freedom to enjoy according to one's ultimate nature is realized without let or hindrance. And those who would block and criticize, who would belittle are no more; and only one great grand experience of the gift of God, the actual, sensing, pulsating, dancing, joy of life remains.

There is a *spiritual* nature to creation, as well as a biological and social nature, to consider next.

V

Life of the Spirit

We are led naturally to the next phase of our thinking, namely, the growth of spirit. What is spirit? It is understood best by analogy. It is that which animates, which makes alive. It is close to enthusiasm in group life, as a source of developing program ideas.

In education we hear the term "school spirit." This is not mere reverence for the alma mater, but an outgoing thing which can be observed at a football game in a crowd of students pulling for their team when it is losing. The school without spirit is listless when being defeated and helpless to turn the tide.

In medicine it is the difference between life and death. It is the doctor who not only knows and uses all the skill of his science, but adds the personal factor of intangible encouragement.

Courage and spirit are closely akin, and the one who encourages literally puts spirit into the one he wants to help. Too much credit cannot be given to encouragement as a vital factor. It may be a source of renewal of vigor and even stimulate the person to generate ideas that may overcome problems which seemed insurmountable.

Courage has been defined as "fear that has said its prayers," and so we come to life of prayer. Prayer is alert relaxation. It is attentive repose. If you observe one in real prayer he may have his eyes closed as if asleep, and yet you know he is not asleep, for there is an air of alertness.

There must always be these two factors alternating. If we are fearful, it is because we do not have faith enough. If we are tense and worried, it is also because of little faith. Faith comes through relaxation. It is like giving ourselves up to the everlasting arms. It is like lying back on the water and floating. The act of trust comes first. One is not sure the water will support him until he tries. We relax through trust.

In regard to fear, it was William Allen White who said, "I do not fear the future because I have seen the past, and I like the present." Fear is balanced by faith. There is no way we can know the future, even though astrologers make a fair living at predicting it.

In the overcoming of the destructive tendency of the mind in criticism, we must constructively try to understand the nature of the critical person. One of the significant ways is to note what the person criticizes. If he criticizes the selfishness of another person, he probably is selfish himself. He projects the quality which he possesses. If he did not have the quality himself, he would likely overlook it in another.

God

It was Josiah Royce, California's gift to American philosophy, who said, "God never sat for a photograph."

Our anthropomorphism is incurable so long as we are "anthropos"—in this state of being, so I am inclined to be not too critical of it. Our views may be even childish like the little girl who asked her mother, "Does God have a skin?" E.S. Brightman in his book, *The Problem of God,* wrote, "God may be a problem to us, and we may be a problem to God. He may be a problem to Himself."

Some picture God as a venerable bookkeeper recording their good and bad deeds. They see God as a judge before whom they will appear on "Judgment Day" for sentencing.

Others picture God in their own likeness as a Caucasian, American, Baptist, Republican. He is on "our side" in any racial, international conflict. I remember an excellent black girl student in Aesthetics saying God was a "black woman."

The idea of God changes with the increase in knowledge

across the centuries. From the early Bible days of the Jealous, to the Judge, to the Righteous, (Elijah, Moses and Isaiah) to the Loving, Caring, Universal (Hosea, Jonah and Jesus) we see the progressive revelation of God.

We may conjecture that not only do we change, but possibly God changes. Just as we profit by experience so God may look on his universal experiments with growing concern. From our limited, infinitesimal perspective, God must at least be a Person and then somehow beyond that. Alfred North Whitehead's God as the "principle of concretion in process" leaves me cold. Process, yes, but Person too. When I try to picture Whitehead's God, it is a giant cement mixer eternally grinding out strips of concrete across time and space! "Principle of concretion" is too impersonal for me as a person. Einstein said he could not understand Whitehead. Whitehead was skeptical of clarity, preferring obscurity. So too is Henry Nelson Wiseman's definition, "God is progressive integration." Perhaps a God defined is a God finished. *Define* means to set limits, to *circumscribe*. *Describe* is a more accurate word. We can write *something* about God, limited by our own stature and comprehension. Henry Moseley said God was the "divine frisky."

In our thoughts we wonder that we cannot apprehend God if he be so all inclusive—by analogy, God is the air we breathe, we look and do not see it—therefore at a glance it does not exist! We do not see the possibility that our sight has not achieved complete perfection. It is because of our own imperfection that we doubt. We do not see the air, but we are always unconsciously living by it.

God appears suddenly to us when we have set the stage expectantly in contemplative prayer, but it was Gandhi who said, "God cannot appear to the starving except in the form of bread."

The existence of God can become an endless debate between those who want to see objectively and touch by hand. "Show us the Father," Philip asks Jesus. He does not *see* that Jesus is doing just that by acting as a son of God. Perhaps the word *existence* needs looking at. It means literally to "stand out."

Thus, as one may be said to stand out from the crowd, he is unmistakable, different. In this sense, Jesus, Buddha, and the saints do "stand out." But we may err in applying that test to God. Wouldn't it be more accurate in our inadequate language to use the word *"essence"*? It avoids the demand for objectivity and yet describes (not defines) an experience we call God. The problem then is the inadequacy of language, certainly nothing to demand an inquisition or burning at the stake of those who *see* God differently with the mind's eye.

Whitehead himself said poets come close to the heart of reality. Einstein, as a scientist, had a deep faith in the rational structure of the universe. He wrote, "Imagination is greater than knowledge. It is the source of all true art and science." So our imaginations are free to conjecture. St. Paul wrote that Jesus is the *Image of God*.

Perhaps the idea is not a container, but a road leading out somewhere. Tomorrow some new idea may be more inclusive. Immanuel Kant wrote, "Two things of which I stand in awe—the starry heavens above and the moral law within." By analogy these indicate God is not only "powerful but good," Ben Franklin said. We can't be too arrogant attempting to "lasso" God.

It may be as A.E. Taylor, the Scottish theologian and philosopher, wrote, "The search for God involves His existence." Increasing knowledge may come from faith. Many scientists attest the fact that their belief in a missing factor led to its discovery.

This leads into the area of spiritual and spiritual discovery. Dag Hammerskjold once wrote, "The longest journey is the journey inward." We may see God in nature; the awe inspiring Grand Canyon may elicit reverence. We may see God in human nature as we witness a sacrificial act of one person for another. Jacob Boehme wrote, "The exterior is the signature of the interior." Boehme tells of "automatic writing" when the creative spirit takes a hold of his hand and guides his writing. The religion of Hinduism finds God in everything, *pantheism*. God is immanent into all, and the process of nature means evolution to higher forms but also devolution to lower forms, depending on the *Karma,* the life lived in each stage.

The philosopher, Charles Hartshorne, has an interesting modification he calls *panentheism,* All is in God rather than God in all.

Buddhism finds the inner journey more significant. God is within, and nothing is worse than being caught on the wheel of things in reincarnation. The inner spirit is released to disappear or perhaps become part of the Eternal Spirit. "The shining dewdrop slips into the silver sea."

Confucius found God in humans, particularly the family; so a person's immortality is in his children, while he as an individual disappears.

In Japan *Shintoism* expanded the family to the state, henotheism.

Moving farther west, the creative spirit manifested itself in a new concept of God, *theism,* as not only immanent in the world but transcendent also. Judaism, inspired with the Egyptian sun worshippers during their sojourn, sublimated the natural to the supernatural God. From the Persian contacts in the later captivity they learned of a God of Darkness, as well as Light, Nuriman and Ahura-Mazda. They added this Prince of Darkness as a powerful competitor of the good God and thus developed the ethics of good and evil.

Christianity used the same concept of *theism.* Various denominations have accented either the transcendence in the more fundamental or immanence in the more liberal churches. churches.

Islam is usually seen as a deistic or totally transcendent idea contrasting to all the other concepts. Islam means to submit to Allah who is totally in control and in five prayer times each person every day seeks to placate Him. It is fatalistic *(Kismet).* What will be happens without personal freedom. The future life is a heaven of rapture and pleasure for those saved by divine grace, and hell for the eternally damned and tortured. This has reminiscence in the hellfire preaching of Jonathan Edwards in American Puritanism, and more recently some evangelists.

Another concept was that of Samuel Alexander of Manchester University in England in his book, *Space-Time and Deity*. He pictures God as the result, the aim of the universal process, and not its instigator in the prime chaos. This might have been inspired by the study of Plato (Timaeus) who writes of four elements in creation, God, the Idea, the Receptacle and Creation. It might be analogous to an artist, model, and studio with materials, and the resulting creation on canvas or sculpture.

The author dealt with his concept of God in the book, *Wise Living*, Stanford Press, 1941. Briefly, *God is wise beneficence*. His nature is power which grows as a result of his creativity, and wisdom which develops with his creativity, but also goodwill (love) in which God is perfect and therefore constant. God works through the natural universe, and the result humans call beauty and truth. Truth is in the nature of the universe, that is how it functions. No one can avoid the truth; we only adhere to it and are happy, or try falsehood and lose. We cannot avoid the earthquake, or other acts of nature, but these are not in themselves malevolent. They are ways in which nature adjusts, and as part of nature so must we. Just so, this which we call "natural evil" is in humans the result of the process of growth. We learn by our mistakes, or should, not to repeat them. Thus we have freedom within limits.

In regard to the immortality concept, there is the obvious material "immortality" of burial and going back as nutrients of Mother earth. There is also "objective" immortality written about by Von Hartmann, who said immortality is what we create, our work lives on for a long or short time. These are possibilities beyond those mentioned in the creative religions.

But there may be an immortality of thought as well as matter. We may in a sense, partially determine it by *the strength and creativity of our thinking*. Perhaps the pessimism of Shakespeare who said, "The evil we do lives on," is not the whole story. Surely the bard's dramas seem to have the mark of immortality in contradiction. They are certainly not evil!

In *Ecclesiastes* 3 we read, "He has made everything beautiful in its time and put eternity in man's mind."

Beauty is transient. The flower fades; the body of the perfect specimen of athlete sags and slows. But in our mind's recesses there is an idea ever beautiful, ever new, the idea of eternity. It gives meaning to the present which Bobby Burns says of the snowfall, " . . . one moment white then melts forever," and Dante, "I will give you beauty for ashes."

It is possible that mental telepathy, which is generally accepted as a fact, may give some indication of immortality. In our fantasy thinking we picture places and events which we have never experienced in real life. Possibly these could be actual places and events revealed to us. by telepathy. We are somehow "tuning in" on a happening not present to our eyes.

Could this operate in a similar way where no physical body was receiving? Just as the reception does not seem to depend on our physical eyes, perhaps the awareness needs nothing physical. Sight and insight are not the same, and the latter need not depend on the former. Some experiments may indicate that dreams which have no relation to the dreamer's experience may result from mental telepathy of another person! We may in our own way become part of the creative process of our universe, co-artists with God. Plato called God the *Demiurge,* (literally "craftsman") not *Nous* or *Logos.* God is a working, creating artist. He longs to create beauty not as the jealous Zeus of Greek mythology, but as loving and desiring to share his creation. Plato thought we apprehend this beauty because we *participate* in it. Our intellect (reasoning by the left brain) tells *how* the imagination by the right brain can *create.*

Plato also uses the name "father" in another context. God may be beyond these concepts. The *demiurge* may be the servant doing God's will.

What is needed is some new creative insight on the nature of God. The saints used prayer vocal and contemplative as did St. Francis and St. Theresa. Brother Lawrence practiced the presence of God throughout each day. More recently Albert Schweitzer, Howard Thurman, and Allan Hunter followed this tradition. Hunter writes, "Silence is the language of God." Possibly out of being able to listen may come the sign we seek. Jesus said the pure in heart will see God. Perhaps purity will clear our sight.

The Story of Noah

One of the greatest legends of all times is that of Noah. It contains the idea that God, after creating the world, was disappointed by mankind, to whom he had given free will. He decides man has taken the wrong course, and all He can do is destroy the world and start over. It is curious that the legend indicates God needed a family to repopulate all of the species.

And so today if we must pass through a destruction of the universe, we need a Noah. We may be destroyed by fire bombs or disease rather than flood, but the analogy is startling. Our Noah would not be so fortunate as the first Noah in having time to save two of each species. He would have to be an ark himself! What would his mind contain? He would be something of an H.G. Wells character. If he somehow escaped the destruction, by the grace of God, he would have to retain all of the arts and sciences, all the philosophies and religions!

His mind would be encyclopedic by nature. We do know in psychology of "photographic" memories. A person with a photographic memory would be the type to keep for the new world our Sermon on the Mount, our Bagavad Gita, the Republic of Plato, the tragedies of Shakespeare, the Einstein theory, the coloring of a Van Gogh.

Or perhaps the Messiah will come from one of our so-called unenlightened, "uncivilized" areas. Wouldn't it be a paradox if, after 2,000 years of missionaries going to the "savages" from "civilized" nations, these advanced nations only destroyed each other with their know-how, and the backward country, which had learned how to live according to nature and nature's God, reversed the process and sent a teacher to the dying civilization to help us out of *our* predicament?

Our faith in this creative, Messianic creature is such that, when the ultimate danger arises, he will make his presence known. When the possible oblivion of the race becomes imminent there will be those who break with the way of the world. From them will come the Messiah.

There is much talk of the possibility of destroying all life on the earth. Leading scientists are pointing out that this danger is not remote. Perhaps from the scientists themselves will come the Messiah. However, a scientist who fulfilled the expectations of this role would have to be a person of profound moral sensitivity. The personalist in philosophy is concerned with taking all the findings of all the sciences and applying them to people. The scientist is not always concerned whether a discovery is bad or good for humanity. He is just as interested in destructive plants and weeds as he is in the crop of the farmer. There is no "good" or "bad" for him, except as it is a good specimen of a weed, for example. There is need for the personal scientist or philosopher who introduces human values into the process of knowledge. It was Kant, the greatest of the modern philosophers, who said:

"I am an investigator by inclination. I feel a great thirst for knowledge and an impatient eagerness to advance, also satisfaction at each progressive step forward. There was a time when I thought that all this could constitute the honor of humanity, and I despised the common people who know nothing about it. Rousseau set me straight. This dazzling excellence vanishes. I learn to honor men, and would consider myself much less useful than common laborers if I did not believe that this purpose gives all others their value . . . to establish the rights of humanity."

Who Survives?

When some writers tell of survival of the fittest, it usually means the most powerful, violent, and vicious. But Darwin himself wrote, "In numberless animal societies the struggle between separate individuals for the means of existence disappears; struggle is replaced by cooperation." They share the space, water, and air.

Peter Farb of The Ecological Society, former editor of *Harpers Series on Nature,* says, "Recent studies of the struggle (for existence) suggest that cooperation and interdependence may be more important for survival of a species than conflict."

All species have mechanisms for limiting conflict. Even the wolf bares his throat when losing to a rival and is not killed.

Tyrannosaurus Rex, the most fearsome of species, has been

extinct for 70 million years. He weighed about 15 tons, was 55 feet long, 20 feet high with 3 foot jaw and 6 inch teeth. There are various theories for his extinction—climate change, geological change, flood, and extra-terrestrial meteor-rain.

The armor plated dinosaurs ruled the earth for 140 million years, but man less than 4 million. The largest (ultrasaurs) were 80 feet long, weighing 80 tons, but had small brains.

When we compare this brain of one pound with the gentle dolphins, whose brain is 40% larger than humans, the picture of survival likelihood is impressive. Dr. John Lilly, who during his 12 years of work with dolphins was never attacked, found that their ethics was one of interdependence. Dr. Lilly says "humans" must learn this humility of dependence on others to survive. Our pride forces us to independence, competition, and conflict. They do not allow warfare or even anger and hostility in their young. They apparently know humans kill them, yet they are friendly. Will they survive us and our mad competition for weapons of human destruction?

John Lilly believes we have to forego our plastic "civilization," always seeking consensus. If so, dissentient creative thinking would lead to a brain development in self-discovery. It may be that we will find *mind evolves from brain in a mystical even spiritual way.*

Dr. Paul Ehrlich maintains that Loris, the 40 million year old primate ancestor of anthropoids, was non-violent, and even more violent anthropoids may have been responding to a hostile environment rather than living violence in their games.

Pygmies in the Rain Forest have no words for *evil, enemy, weapon,* or *war,* living in harmony with nature which they love. They believe the forest is divine. Native Tahitians discourage conflict in their children as an illness, which God inflicts on haters. (This sounds much like Dr. Jonas Salk who writes that those who defend violence are emotionally ill.)

Other examples are the aborigines of Australia, the Hopi and Zuni Indians who live a communal life with no violence or wars. On the other hand, the Apaches and Comanches encourage in their children, aggression, competition, conflict, and even killing. Could our early code of the West with its revenge, hatred and killing be the American choice of survival? Beating the devil out of children by adults who believe in original sin creates resentment which in later life leads to violence toward others.

"Quick on the draw" is a test of reflex, not cortex. It takes no brains, no thought process to shoot quickly. That which distinguishes higher forms of evolution is their development of the cortex, which presents the human with the possibility of choice when confronted with a strange situation. There is no alternative to reflex. It's kill or be killed. This is the principle taught in the military, shoot first, then ask questions. The lack of handgun control in America, largely due to the strong lobby in Congress of the National Rifle Association, is a national disgrace. Our stories and motion pictures make for good guys and bad guys.

Any two value systems result in polarization and thus eventual confrontation. There is no alternative which would be provided by intelligence. A further serious difficulty with this is that the reflex only means that outside events will control us. We just react to a situation instead of controlling it by intellect's free choice. Thus the person is demeaned; there is less concern for the other person. It was the Jewish philosopher, Martin Buber, who wrote, "Treat every other person as a Thou, never as an it."

What are some examples of alternatives in conflict situations? Instead of the one way of reflex which means elimination or extermination, cortex offers the non-violence of marches, sit-ins and boycotts. A second area is in the subtle psychology of undermining morale, a passive resistance. A third area is by civil disobedience, such as the refusal to pay taxes. Henry Thoreau, a century ago, used this last way when he disapproved of our invasion of Mexico. Even some of the Catholic soldiers refused to fire on the Mexican Catholics and were publicly branded with a "D" on their cheeks as deserter.

In any event, we may find our humanity best realized and survival assured through non-violence.

Joseph

What a man this must have been! Matthew mentions him first as a "just man," because he wanted to shield Mary from possible disgrace of a pregnancy before they had consummated their marriage. In the eyes of the Jewish law, her pregnancy amounted to a reason for divorce, yet Joseph was magnanimous beyond the letter of the law.

His influence on Jesus in childhood and youth must have been remarkable. Why else could the young man Jesus think of God as a father? Certainly Jesus had no knowledge of Plato, who spoke in those terms. If God was like a father, the example of Joseph as a father must have been most impressive.

It was for Jesus to develop the concept of the fatherhood of God into the international God beyond the Jewish state of Israel, a God of all people. They followed the logical, but daring, conclusion that all mankind was part of one family, the brotherhood of man. This stroke of genius may have had its inception in the character of Joseph.

The only other mention of him is his and Mary's concern when Jesus remained in the temple after their company had left to return home. They thought he was lost.

Apparently Joseph died before the Crucifixion, for only Mary was present.

Jesus and the Church

"The institution is the lengthened shadow of a great man."

An institution is not only the lengthened shadow; it is the static structure. It is a shadow of reality, the reality of creative man. It contains no breath of life. It may even suffocate creative life. When men give their loyalty to it, and not to life, it frustrates them. Its purpose is the secret of its sinister character. It seeks to sustain itself at all costs, even to the detriment of life and living things. It is the tomb of the spirit.

A Modern Parable

Jesus came to a place the people called the church. It was a grand edifice with towering spire and massive buttresses. Jesus asked again what it was called, for He had a word like it in His time, and then it meant a very different thing. Some of His disciples had gone on tours and called the people to repent of their sins and live His way. These people were called *ecclesia*, the church. But this was a building, static, and ponderous, not a living, moving being.

Jesus was puzzled, but it was not His nature to condemn, and particularly not to pass judgment without investigation. So He went up to the huge doors, and He pushed on one. It did not yield. He tried another and another. All were locked. He turned to us in wonder, and we tried to explain. "They open the doors on Sunday, the first day of each week. It is open one day in seven, and the people come, at least some of the people of the city come, to hear music and are urged by one whom they pay to urge them. Sometimes this paid person becomes vehement in urging them to repent, and they get another who speaks more melodiously in his place."

"But," Jesus remonstrated, "today is Sunday, is it not?"

"Yes, but the church is only open for an hour or so in the morning and occasionally in the evening," we countered.

Jesus looked up at the spire and then turned away toward the city. We heard him say quietly, "It is just as well. A sepulcher should be seldom opened."

The next day, being concerned to learn more of Jesus' attitude toward our church, we pressed Him for other words about it. He was sympathetic and gentle as He said, "It is possible that the meaning of words change with the centuries. So with the word *church;* it formerly meant a group of people who were called by an inner voice to live after my way. But now it means a place and not a state of being. This might be all right," He reasoned as He taught us.

"It is possible, if the church be regarded as a place, to conceive it as wherever the spirit of good will dwells. To try to capture the spirit and imprison it in a certain kind of building is to misunderstand the nature of goodness. It is possible for a great multitude of people to meet for an hour once a week in the building we saw yesterday and have the spirit of good will. It is also possible for a solitary farmer to have it in a stable, or a lone shepherd out under the sky. But the important thing is not the place. It is the spirit which can live any place.''

The next day we inquired further of Jesus in regard to the nature of this spirit. And he said, ''The spirit is that which animates, that which sparkles in children's eyes, that which warms the hearts of weary travelers, that which blesses the aged, that which endures beyond the body, in other physical forms.''

A good example of one who tried to put the teachings of Jesus to work was that of Vincent Van Gogh. He studied Methodism in England while teaching languages when he was only 23 years of age. He wanted to be a minister but failed the exams. He went to Belgium to a dismal place called the Borinage where coal miners lived in near poverty. He shared life in their homes and also in the mines, he dressed as they did, ate the same fare and nursed the sick and taught children. He gave away his salary, most of his clothes and possessions, even his bed. He defended them when they went on strike against the inhuman conditions, and for this he was relieved of the post and forbidden to preach by the church authorities, who said he was ''disgracing the ministry'' by his poor dress and identifying himself with the miners. He tried to lose himself in his art, but he could not find fulfillment and so he turned to suicide.

The poet, Elinor Lennen wrote, ''Allan Hunter gave the church horizons for its walls.''

The Good Samaritan

One of the most incisive stories of the application or disregard of ''practicing what we preach'' is this story.

It was tested in 1973 by psychologists J. Darley and C. Batson at a theological seminary. At different times, each of 40 students was assigned to deliver a sermon on ''The Good Samaritan,'' or ''Job Opportunities for Seminarians'' at a place across the campus. On the way, each came upon a person in great distress and groaning (an actor). Those who stopped (16 of the 40) were equally divided on their sermon subjects, showing their behavior had no relation to their expressed religiosity!

All of which is exactly the point Jesus made. The priest, the Levite, and the Samaritan, an enemy of the Jews, were examples of ethical action or inaction. The religionists were not practicing their religion while the foreigner was good without any religious reason. This type of story infuriated the Jewish leaders.

Let us imagine a modern situation to give perspective. Suppose a minister is driving the freeway when he observes an auto accident with the victim needing first aid. But he is on his way to a funeral and must tell of the sacrificial life of a woman who always helped those in need. He keeps going.

Next the church custodian comes by. He also sees the predicament of the victim but is late in setting up the chairs for the service at church. He keeps going.

Who is the most despised, hated, feared person today? A Mexican farm laborer? A Communist? An Iranian? Choose your own worst enemy, and picture him stopping to help your wife and child hurt in an accident.

What Is It That Dies?

All wrongdoing is taking a mistaken way toward a goal of all life. The tragedy of sin is not the condemnation of the saintly; it is that it dies.

One can choose to live forever. One's immortality is self-determined. There is no way that showing the right spirit, forgiving, and loving can die. It is creating a right spirit by every act of kindness, consideration, sacrifice; it is building a soul.

"Wrong" ideas are those which won't work, which can't succeed. So wrong ways of treating others fail. They disappear.

"Righteous" indignation, and "justifiable" anger are projections of the dying spirit. They are attempts to excuse anger and criticism. They are the last gasps of the wrong spirit, of ill will.

The Future of Sin

Sin has no future. In the very nature of the universe it cannot endure. It is like sweeping back the tides. The real definition of good is that which lasts, that which partakes of the Eternal. The longer it lasts the better it is.

Sin is the residue of the evolutionary process toward the ideal. It is that which is discarded, which won't work toward a goal. "It is henceforth good for nothing but to be cast out and trampled underfoot," or burned up.

Sin means to "miss the mark," that is, to misunderstand the meaning of life, to aim at the target but not to succeed, to take the wrong road while thinking it is the right road. It does not mean deliberately doing the wrong thing. That is why Jesus spent his time with "sinners," showing them a better way to live, how to *hit* the mark.

Sin is to the moral order what excrement is to physical growth. It is the unused material of moral growth.

Faith, Hope and Love

"I may have absolute faith to move mountains but if I have no love I count for nothing," says Paul in one of the most impressive tributes to love, *I Corinthians* 13. We have already commented on its similarity to Plato's Symposium speech of Agathon, which might have been its inspiration. Although Agathon does not use the word *savior,* Paul deals with love in the context of faith, a religious term foreign to Greek thought.

From the distinction of faith, Paul continues by comparing love also to charity. Just the act of giving is possible without love, as one would thus save on income tax today. James later wrote, "Faith without work is dead."

It is difficult not to find love in sacrifice. Paul clarifies the definition of love by recounting what it is: patient, kind; not jealous, proud, rude, selfish, irritated or resentful. It is not gladdened by wrong but by goodness, slow to expose, eager to believe the best, hopeful and eternal.

I am glad he included hope which tends to be overlooked in sermons today. These anxious times need hope, the positive, encouraging work. Paul concludes, "faith, hope and love, but the greatest is love."

Perhaps these three words illustrate the Greek cyclical theory of time. Will Durant titles one of his books on the Story of Civilization, *The Age of Faith,* preceding the Renaissance and Reformation. With all the tension and constant threat of chemo-nuclear disaster hanging over us, could this "age of anxiety" be a dawn of an "age of hope"?

Do we dare to hope for an age of love, not just romantic, but the love that Plato and Jesus spoke of?

Let us reflect on the task of philosophers.

VI

The Task of Philosophers

Much of the modern philosophers thinking has been preoccupied with finding out what their job is. Like Archimedes they are trying to find "a place to stand." They may not be fascinated by his goal of "moving the world," but they do want a reason for living.

Since Kant, the last of the great creative thinkers, the professional philosophers have pursued two trails, one, logical analysis, and the other existentialism. Have these led to their goals?

The logicians have been trying to clarify the meaning of words, searching for a common denominator, so they can understand one another. In trying to simplify, they have resorted to mathematics and physics. But Carnap's equations and Reichenbach's claim to finding the answer in *The Rise of Scientific Philosophy* are reminiscent of the ancient philosopher crying, "Eureka" in the bathtub! Reichenbach, a friend of Einstein, and himself a theoretical physicist, looked at the philosophers of history, Hegel *et al.*, finding them irrelevant. In looking at history and literature in the humanities, they become historians and poets. Thus they disappear as philosophers with a unique task.

But in trying to make philosophy scientific by focusing on the problems of science, Reichenbach went to the other extreme and really remained a scientist, not finding the task of philosophy. This impoverished the language and thus curiously led to less understanding when it eliminated shades of meaning.

The second trail has also led to a dead end. *Existentialism* with its emphasis on the moment, the only thing that *exists*, has no place to stand to gain perspective on the passing show of moments. It is like a motion picture made up of a succession of instant snapshots. It lacks reason for living which is the goal of modern philosophers. Existence with no consideration of essence, the present without the ultimate, the moment without eternity tells us nothing.

What then is the task of philosophers? Speculation yes, but not researching and grubbing in past events. Santayana has never been challenged in his pontifical edict, "If man does not learn from history, he is condemned to repeat it." The truth is, we never can repeat history. New situations create new problems. Reichenbach started on the right trail but got sidetracked in the parsimony of physics. He had little knowledge or even thought about psychology and the social sciences, and this is *where the problems today are*.

While there are past events in history which have some semblance to the present, they are also different. An old friend who spent many years in the federal government told me once that the govenment works, or in many cases fails to work, on the basis of *precedent*. For example, the earliest decision of the State department proceeded to the second decision to set up a line which determined the direction of the third decision, and so on up to the present. This dogma of procedure stultifies the process of solving new issues. The United Nations, representatives of many nations, in its summer conference on disarmament failed to find new ways because of this problem.

The philosopher will find plenty to do, a task in creative thinking on such problems as the nuclear threat. This sword of Damocles hangs over humanity as the major problem of our day. It is new, because the advent of the nuclear age was not presaged in history, logical analysis, or existentialism. If the problem is not solved there will be no need to think of others. They dwarf into triviality.

A major enigma of our days is the silence of higher education on this problem. It points up the nature of academia, which *lags* behind the present because of vested interests of professors pursuing their pet research project. Some of them even become agents of the military industrial complex because it is financially profitable, while seeking solutions to the ethical, social problem is not. Robert J. Lifton of Yale writes, "We have to acknowledge the scandal that the central issue of our time has been fundamentally ignored in our universities. There is very little discussion of nuclear threat."

No one enjoys reading the history of philosophy more then I. Plato's exposition of Socrates' dialogs puncturing egos of sophists is a good basis for the democracy of the town meeting where the input of each person aids in finding the truth of a practical issue. It is an example of cooperative thinking which could well be emulated by the academia of our time in working together of all the disciplines in solving the major issues. When the American Association of University Professors was founded in 1915, John Dewey was elected President. Two standing committees were organized: (1) Academic Freedom and Tenure, (2) Academic Obligations. The first met regularly but the second never met. This may be one indication of where the academic community is thinking.

Haven and Lodestar
A philosopher is one who looks at life, finds it serious business, demanding thought, and decides his course accordingly. He who finds this action inevitable from the start has the philosophic temper as a birthright. He is instinctively the thinker and has one obsession, the "eternal why?" It is this individual who was puzzled from the start about life, as though he had lived elsewhere and suddenly mysteriously found himself in a different universe. His feeling must be something like that described in H.G. Wells' *Men Like Gods*, when a party of five, speeding along a glassy highway in a high-powered motor car, suddenly strike the fourth dimension and find themselves in a new world.

This intuition that the eternal has thus entered time brings the born philosopher a uniquely beautiful interpretation of life itself.

Wordsworth wrote:

> "But trailing clouds of glory do
> we come
> From God, who is our home."

This element is sadly needed in our humdrum existence. It gives tone and meaning to going on. David Grayson tells how much he needed it in his *Adventures in contentment*. He had been so involved in the rush of life that a time came when he gave up the race and sank inert. Out of this came his beautiful philosophy of taking time to look up at the stars with a friend, or down at warm Mother Earth to feel the security of her buoyancy. Before that his only thought had been a strenuous obsession, the exhausting American creed of "getting ahead."

So Philosophy has a dual task. For the youth about to embark, it provides a lodestar to guide. Sir James Barrie in his commencement address to the graduates of the University of Edinburgh said in part:

"They said to us of old, 'Hitch your wagon to a star.' The tragedy of your day is that there are no more wagons, and, so some say, no need for stars. But I trust, you will pitch your ladder against the stars and climb your highest."

Walt Whitman in *Passage to India* puts it:

> "Sail forth, steer for the deep waters only,
> we will risk the ship, ourselves and all."

And then there are those of the quiet years who have embarked from the mainland of the soul and set out with the lodestar as a guide long ago. But they had some stormy going in high seas. From birth the philosophic temper had them very sensitive, and life hurt them terribly. And again philosophy came to their rescue. As of old it had provided a challenge to go forth and meet life in its abundance, so now it beckons to a haven secure from the raw winds which cut thin blood of age.

To Prometheus stretched painfully under blistering sun on barren rock it came:

> "Night shall come with its garniture of stars
> to comfort thee with shadows."

Star and shadow are symbols in this our present universe of a source that is the eternal and a future that presages life triumphant. How egotistical of a mortal to hold blatantly that the *élan vital*, the life force, dies with him! Man's Divine Origin and glorious fate cannot be taken from him. It is part and destiny of the very nature of living things.

Patience, Persistence and Persuasion

The task of the peacemaker requires attention to the way it's done, the manner of the approach and conducting the dialog. In the past too little attention has been paid to the technique of reconciliation.

Over anxiety about achieving the goal may lead to exacerbating the problem. If we really want to win and solve it, there are at least three requirements.

The first is *patience*. This means being a good *listener*. To rush in with ready made answers, or even employ what has been successful in past situations, may not be the successful way in the new situation. There are new persons with new backgrounds, possibly different cultures, which first must be understood. The least we say the better, because every word will have different meanings to the new persons and their interpretation of it. Time is required and probably more than one dialog between the persons involved. This means *persistence,* the second requirement. If at first we don't succeed, try again, and again—.

Another reason for it is that the parties to the dispute at their deepest level want it settled and they have an admiration and appreciation, perhaps not shown, for the tenacity of the reconciler. He never gives up hope.

Then the third requirement is *persuasion*. Often this is attempted too early in the process. It works best when all the sides are heard and understood. Then only can an attempt to modify positions be approached.

> "Convinced against his will
> He's of the same opinion still."

VII

The Compulsion
Of the Muse

There seems to be a drive from birth in the artist which becomes an obsession to produce. It relates to the history of the race and primitive art. Yet it seems to arrive in a particular development in certain starstruck individuals. It is unique, God given. We call it Homer, Phidias, Aeschulus, Sophocles, Michelangelo, Da Vinci, Mozart, Beethoven, Tchaikovsky, Shakespeare, Milton, Browning, Emerson, Van Gogh, Cézanne, as the case may be.

It bursts forth uninhibited as a bird song. It "trails clouds of glory." It is automatic writing, using the artist only as an instrument. It finds him neither self-effacing or self-deprecatory. It leaves him neither puffed up nor regal. It is transient yet eternal, present yet evanescent. It is not affected by what others say, by the art critic, self-appointed, or aesthetic theorist. Above all it is direct, honest, and genuine. It is unmistakably real yet sublime. It may be in the air all about us, yet only some have the mystical touch to react and grasp it for all to suddenly see, hear, and touch. That is the mark of genius, the signature of the divine. Freud said the great artist was a complex mystery before whom the analyst must lay down his arms.

The beauty of creativity is that it is problem-solving in a non-violent way. Georges Braque, the French artist, at one time in his life was so poor he couldn't buy paints and canvas, but the compulsion to create was so great, he gathered bits of colored paper, scraps and fallen leaves and pasted them together.

Thus out of the compulsion he created a new form of art, the collage. Problems of relations with others and within the self yield to art.

Children's play may be innovative, solving questions. A stage play is possibly a drama working on solution to an issue. Erik Erikson, the analyst said creativity is a sign of health—the maturing integration of character. The writings which follow are evidences of the compulsion on the author of this book. They are his attempt at creativity.

Mountain and Sea

The mountain and I never grow tired
of each other

—Li Po (701-62 A.D.)

From the flat lands of Northern Illinois where the highest hills were Indian mounds of the Sauk tribes, to the majestic splendor of snow-capped San Gorgonio, "old Grayback," what a revelation! I have never ceased to wonder. And then there's Mount San Antonio, nicknamed "old Baldy" with his crown of eternal snow. From our home in Pasadena, it was plainly visible in 1913, and when I taught at Upland College fifty years later it stood just above us, still overwhelming to contemplate.

And "contemplation" seems the appropriate word, a wonder akin to reverence, which has never escaped me. I think of Li Po, 1200 years ago, with the same feeling, as he gazed at the Himalayas, 10,000 miles from me! China's greatest poet found inspiration for his Taoist meditations on *The Way*.

Then I saw the sea, the Pacific, when as teenagers we went to the beach for swimming. What a contrast! The sea seemed endless to the horizon, joining the sky. It was incomprehensible, constantly moving, a never ceasing ebb and flow. Unlike the mountain it seemed restless, unhappy, disturbed and disturbing. Serenity "calmness of spirit" comes from the same root as "calm sea," but I have never experienced that calmness.

On the other hand, the mountain is constant, dependable, even when attacked by storm and wind.

Moses found it the source of abiding law, and Jesus found freedom from temptations of mind, body, and political power.

The Condor

One of the most ugly, if not the ugliest, bird is the condor. He, when perched and motionless, looks like a prehistoric monstrosity and altogether frightful!

And then by strange metamorphosis the condor leaves the land for its true element, the insubstantial air, and becomes a creature of entrancing beauty. No wonder we are trying to prevent its extinction.

And so may it not be with us? Earthbound may seem to be our nature with all of its gravity pull downward, misshapping our ends. But we can overcome and outfly our night to become a part of radiant beauty as the moth who wings directly into the flame, disappearing, yet a bit of reality absorbed in the Eternal.

Response

A small boy wandered up in the hills to unknown heights. As he went, the canyon loomed ahead and the shadows came as the day drew to a close.

He lost his way and became fearful. His terror grew as the night came, and he shouted out in terror—"I'm afraid!" To his amazement an echo came back—"I'm afraid!"

He was not alone. Some one was answering!

"I'm glad you are here," brought the same words back to him, and his fears were dissipated. He lay down to sleep.

In the morning he woke, and the sun was streaming down the canyon, showing him the way. As the boy made his way, he expressed his gratitude—"I love you!" which brought back—"I love you."

Chieko

Tom met her by luck as they watched the football game from the bleachers. They both enjoyed cheering and the enthusiasm of the crowd. Tom looked at her out of the corner of his eye. He liked her smile, particularly, and found the eyes attractive. It wasn't as if there weren't plenty of girls on campus, but he never seemed to find one just right. He asked her name "Chieko—what's yours?"—"Tom."—and it seemed just right. She was something special.

Chieko was pleasantly surprised to be noticed and obviously a bit taken by his being Caucasian. Relations between races, to put it mildly, had been strained, largely due to native prejudices and consequent Japanese restraint and reserve. People on the Coast had not welcomed the Chinese and subjected them to ridicule as "pigtails." But the railroads had needed them in the early construction days.

As for the Japanese, coming later, they were mostly truck gardeners with small patches of land they farmed. They were maligned as "skibbies." Of course Tom was aware of this, although his family was not given to making fun of others. There was only one black boy in the high school who therefore seemed no threat. He accepted the role they gave him as campus clown, even though it was degrading at times. One must survive.

Through all of this, the churches had been an ameliorating influence. First generation Japanese parents, anxious for their American born children to get on well, sent them to Sunday Schools, and occasionally when they received a genuine welcome actually joined the church, attended services, and supported it financially as their fortune favored.

Chieko had first hand experience of prejudice in her own family. Her older brother, Gene, a senior on the high school debate team, entered an Oratorical contest on American Democracy sponsored by a local newspaper. He was so outstanding there was no doubt about the winner, and the judges awarded him. The newspaper would send him to Washington D.C., to compete in a national contest. At this point the principal interceded saying no person of foreign extraction could represent this high school in such a contest. Accordingly he awarded the prize to the second place "American" boy. He in turn went to Washington and won the National contest!

Tom, of course, knew about this, as he and Chieko were in

the Junior Class. Nothing was said of it between them as their friendship grew. Tom had the temerity to take her home to visit with his parents. They were most hospitable, and his sister was delighted at this unique situation. Chieko, in turn, invited him to dinner with her family where he met Gene for the first time.

It was coming on toward the Christmas holidays and suddenly it was December 7th! Tom and his family heard President Roosevelt declare a state of war. Chieko with her family heard it too. California panicked from the Governor on down. With the fleet of Pearl Harbor destroyed, all sorts of rumors spread. Japanese submarines were seen off the Coast, receiving signals from traitors in this country. The tenuous relations of the races, never too certain, evaporated.

But Tom had much to talk over, and there was much she wanted to tell him. The threatened relation brought them even closer instead of separating. Chieko said Gene had volunteered, and a Japanese battalion was being formed, the 442nd American to serve in Italy. Tom was voicing his concern that she and her folks not be subjects of the community's attack as the fear and suspicion increased.

Then came the presidential decree. All citizens of Japanese descent were to be evacuated from the Pacific Coast. There had been no verified case of disloyalty on the part of any of them. Even Hawaii out in the Pacific, and much more vulnerable, made no such discrimination. But relocation centers were set up in the Rocky Mountain states and as far east as Chicago.

Chieko and her folks were stoic in their preparation to leave. Gene was already gone to training camp for the Army. Tom and his parents were helpless in their friendship. They invited Chieko and her folks to a farewell dinner, a sad occasion indeed. Tom's sister was in tears most of the evening.

Chieko's family was ordered to the Santa Anita racetrack in Arcadia to await further notice. Tom couldn't sit still. Although Caucasians were forbidden admittance except for the military surveillance, he got through a jockey's entrance hidden from the public for their protection. He found in some cases two families quartered in one stall. The odor left by the horses was unpleasant and the air cold with lack of heat. His dexterity in avoiding the guards finally brought him to Chieko's family. It was heartrending to see their condition, yet they were trying to make the best of it. Imprisonment is not only taking one's freedom, but false imprisonment is morally degrading and saps the spirit. Tom saw it dying in her father's eyes and was enraged at what he saw around him. All they had was what they could carry. Most of their possessions had been sold to friends or in some cases sharp buyers. The California real estate dealers who had lobbied for the relocation were to make millions before the whole thing was over.

Tom and Chieko whispered farewells as he held her close. Chieko would write as soon as they reached their destination and had an address. Leave-taking was ended, and Tim slipped out into the darkness past the guards. When he returned home, his folks were anxious not only for their Japanese friends, but Tom's risk and possible detection. The church would keep in touch with the "relocation centers" (American for concentration camp) and send all needed aid.

The wait for word seemed interminable. The Japanese families were sent, by train, to their new location. Chieko's letter came and Tom was waiting for the delivery. It was from Heart Mountain, Wyoming. He read every word over and over. The housing was poor at best with tarpaper siding offering little protection in the spring cold air. They prayed for summer and a chance to get out and plant a little garden. Fresh vegetables were in short supply, and the government was investing in guns not butter, particularly for suspects. But the high altitude and cold were the chief hardships particularly for Southern Californians. Chieko kept busy with her Senior Class studies, but the folks had little to occupy the time. Her mother tried to keep busy with cooking and mending clothes. The church had sent them warm clothes which was a godsend after the little they brought with them. The men gathered and talked politics. Some, more daring in demanding their rights as citizens, were sent to Tule Lake Camp for troublemakers.

Chieko's folks had heard from Gene who was about to go overseas with his outfit. The irony of it all was not lost when he told his bitterness at fighting for his country while it falsely imprisoned his family. Such is freedom in wartime. He felt he must prove himself in battle as his only means of showing the nation and the world. It was not long before he would get his chance in Italy.

Tom wrote a long letter to Chieko about every bit of what was happening at high school in his Senior year. But he said his imagination was with her at Heart Mountain. What a cynical name for her place! At least his heart was there and not in his studies.

Their correspondence was a lifesaver for both. Each shared his deepest feelings with each other. As Chieko told of the suffering, physical and spiritual, Tom's plans began to take shape. He must register for the draft soon. His course of action was determined not only by his church upbringing with its teachings of Jesus on love and nonviolence, but he wanted to share at least some of what Chieko was enduring. He registered finally as a conscientious objector, expecting either to be denied that status and go to prison, or be recognized and sent to a camp perhaps similar to Chieko's.

The local draft board denied his petition, even refusing to grant him a hearing. This refusal, to their chagrin, gave Tom the legal right for an appeal to the Department of Justice for a hearing. This was granted and the Hearing Officer after several hours of questioning granted him status. He was sent to a Civilian Public Service Camp, not unlike the Civilian Conservation Corps camps at Waldport on the Oregon Coast. He was satisfied and packed to go. It was early winter and though the Northern Coast is not as cold as the Rockies, there was plenty of rain and fog during the winter.

Tom wrote to Chieko of his new life and work. He was under the Forestry Service, not the military, during the work day, and the camp was one organized for CO's by the Brethren Service Committee. Quakers and Mennonites also provided camps. The churches had a minister as Director who administered the camp with the men selecting their own leaders democratically. Tom was one of the youngest campers, most of whom were midwest farm boys, a few Mexican-Americans, and some college men. Most of the officers elected were from the last group. All of this he wrote to Chieko. It helped vitiate the pain of his empathy for her, and he hoped that it would give her a feeling that she was not alone. Distance did make the heart grow fonder for both of them.

The winter seemed interminable for Tom. The rains came and came and came! Chieko wrote of the suffering of the people in one of the most frigid winters on record. Thermometers went down to 20° below, but the ceaseless winds from the Arctic brought the wind chill factor to 50° and 60° below.

As winter passed Chieko's resistance was low and she came down with pneumonia. Unable to write, her mother sent Tom the bad news and asked for his prayers. He was frantic. He could go A.W.O.L. and try to get there. But he would be caught, put in prison, even farther from seeing her.

The infirmary at Heart Mountain was inadequate at best, and the doctor available was handicapped not only by lack of equipment but by having no specialization. He applied to superiors to have her moved to the closest available hospital in Cody, 100 miles East. Going through channels of authority who couldn't care less took too long, and Chieko was gone.

Tom never fully recovered. Authorities could give leave of absence for a "death in the immediate family," but that was denied him. As his bitterness subsided, he thought he would rather remember her as alive, vibrant, sparkling.

At last the war was over, and he and Chieko's family could return home. He loved them as his own folks. Theirs was a double blow for Gene had been sent home with a loss of an arm. Unlike Chieko, he had received the best medical assistance. His battalion, the 442nd, all Japanese, was the most decorated in American history, and he had proven himself in action.

The anomaly and the paradox are beyond explanation. The freedom Gene fought for was denied his own loved ones!

As for Tom, the dull aching void stayed with him, for his nature was steadfastness in loyalty to Chieko.

Old Fletcher's Last Ride

He was late! He looked at Prince accusingly. Why hadn't he wakened him? The dog hung his head to the side with a pleading look for forgiveness. He had looked up at the alarm clock at the exact moment of 1:45 P.M., when it always sent up a frightful racket. But . . .nothing.

The old man looked from the dog to the clock. He must hurry! He pulled on his pants and shirt, grabbed his old stick, and was out the door with Prince close behind. The royal title was strange to the mongrel, but the old man looked on him not as he was, but as a thoroughbred. The dog sensed his honor and was forever trying to live up to it.

The first time he had ever been late to salute the Chief! He must make it. He quickened his pace to a jerky ramble which belied his age. The old Santa Fe station was three blocks away and the Chief was always on time—2:15 P.M.

Bob Gillford was leisurely returning to the office after lunch at home. He was the town's highly respected young lawyer. People said he'd be mayor one of these days. Bob saw the little drama on the sidewask as he drove along. The anxiety of the old man was apparent to him and he drew along the curb. "How about a lift, Mr. Fletcher?"

"Yer just in time," exclaimed the old man, "a real answer to prayer," as they heard the Chief's whistle in the distance. Prince jumped eagerly in the back seat.

The Chief no longer made a stop at the small town, but it slowed up some. "We can just make it to the station in the car. Bob, yer a life saver!" The car picked up quickly under Bob's ready response to the emergency note in the old man's voice. Then it suddenly dawned on Bob that this was the only diversion old Fletcher had. It was his reason for living. Every day he stood at attention, and then as the engineer waved, he saluted his cane as a sword. This colorful ceremony had gone on ever since Fletcher retired far back in the past. No one knew his age, but it must certainly have been in the nineties.

They hit the driveway to the platform and out scrambled old Fletcher just as the train pulled along. The old man beamed as the engineer acknowledged his raised cane by a sharp whistle, his hand extended from the cab. What a thrill! Bob left, a catch in his throat, and fell to musing as he returned to the office.

A few days later his musing brought together a few townsfolk including the station agent. He was stubborn in answer to Bob's proposal at first. No train ever did such a thing, schedules and all, you know. But the station agent had formed a tremendous attachment to old Fletcher too. He didn't know what it would be like not to see that welcome figure hobble up the platform every day—rain, snow, or shine. It wouldn't hurt to contact the Chicago main office, in any case. They could say no, and the townsfolk would have to subside again.

But no one knows the powers above, and the ways of the world. When the request came, it found J.D. Romser in a benign mood. Hadn't he just got the government contract, as the railroad was sagging with dark days ahead? The idea suddenly caught his imagination; maybe this was just that personal touch, what the road needed to get people interested in train travel again! The jets had certainly hurt railroad business, with their personal service emphasis. He scribbled an O.K. on the bottom of the letter, and the wheels were rolling for old Fletcher. The station agent looked in amazement when the O.K. came through. He dialed the wrong number for Bob's office, and when he did get Bob he became the voice of official authority. Yes, his (the station agent's) request "as usual" had been okayed; their plans could go ahead.

Days went by and old Fletcher had the alarm clock working and made all appointments at the station. Then came a Sunday. And a perfect day it was, he thought, as he started out; how perfect, he didn't realize until later. As he got within a block of the station, it seemed everyone in town was there. "Could they all be coming this way from Church?" he wondered. He quickened his hop step to the platform where the crowd had gathered. Must be someone important, maybe a senator or even the President, coming through on the Chief. He hadn't been reading the paper lately; his eyes were bothering him, and his spectacles were no good anymore.

He heard the whistle of the Chief and looked down the track. There seemed to be a joyful expectancy everywhere, a holiday. Even the whistle sounded enthusiastic. Yes, here comes the Chief! Fletcher stood ready for salute. The crowd made way for him. What was happening? The Chief was slowing down! Yes, majestically the Chief pulled into the station and came to a complete stop.

Coming toward him were the station manager and a dignified appearing stranger who had swung off the train. He waited, puzzled, and then the manager spoke. "Mr. Fletcher, this is the vice president of the railroad, Mr. J.D. Romser. He has something to tell you."

Old Fletch turned, not knowing what to say. The dignitary spoke with a flourish, well aware of the crowd of people listening. "Mr. Fletcher, we know at the headquarters of your long service and particularly of the constant daily note of good will to the Chief. I am authorized to give you this certificate of appreciation. It authorizes you this day to board the engine of the Chief and ride into the city on pre-arranged, specified dates, when hotel accommodations and entertainment have been arranged for you during the coming week, returning home again in the Chief's engine cab."

The crowd was cheering and old Fletcher's face broke into a grin. "The greatest moment of my life," he responded, as he walked with the vice president to the throbbing engine with all the dignity of the president of the railroad. Once aboard, he looked out of the window at the platform where he had daily stood alone through the years. Now it was completely covered with townsfolk, many of whom he did not know.

As the train pulled away he waved to them in the grand style the engineer had always waved at him. They did not see him slump to the floor of the cab, far down the tracks.

My Indian Summer

Human beings have an Indian summer just as the years have that season. In Northern Illinois it is probably the most beautiful and satisfying time of the year. The leaves turn to golden brown shades and are gathered for bonfires as the early fall days go by. There is then not only the treat for eyes but the delightful odors and sounds of crackling fires. And next the pleasures of taste as marshmallows roasting bring the sense of touch in the sticky sweets.

But even more than the five seasons there is that indefinable subtle intuition that all the world of nature is just right!

As for me, I am suddenly aware of Indian summer in my own days. The slower pace as I withdraw gradually from the academic merry-go-round is welcome. There is more time to pause and listen to a bird song, pat a stray dog, breathe deeply near a rose garden or an orange grove. The pleasure of good food tastefully prepared, and reading a book for sheer curiosity not just class participation, make the season more delightful. We can't "go home again," because we never really left it. It is always with us.

Choosing Memories

One of the interesting pastimes is reminiscing. It can be enjoyable or sad, depending on the time and place of the happening as well as the event itself.

Fortunately, the human being is given by nature the powers of choice. It would be tragic if we had to live over in memory all of the unpleasant and disastrous occurances repeatedly. Some elderly spend much time in this way and their lives reflect that.

But they could reverse the feedback by continually recounting the pleasant times. It brings a mellow geniality which those around enjoy also as they contact them. No one likes to be in the presence of morose and cynical people young or old.

In Proverbs we read, "A merry heart doeth good like a medicine." Laughter is the best medicine, it relieves tension, calms temper. Laugh with others, not at them, particularly those less fortunate.

How to Retire Gracefully

The Rainbow—go out and look for it!
Older friends, visits.
Do for yourself, independent.
Do something for others in need, counseling.
Write.
Look out the window.
Believe in God's will.
Believe in immortality.
Pray.
Keep a daily schedule.
Use the library.
Enjoy T.V. selected shows.
Exercise, walk and swim.
Serenity when you can do nothing about problem.
Example for others of faith.
Thanksgiving and praise God.
Forget slights and injustices.
Teach every chance you get, for that has been your joy.

Song of the Sioux

Out of the village at dawn
Ride the braves to attack—
Song of the Sioux crying!

Out of the wigwam at noon
Squaws seek signs of the braves—
Song of the Sioux sighing.

Out of the dusk at eve
Limp the last of the long knives—
Song of the Sioux dying.

(Note: After the defeat of Custer at Little Big Horn 1876, the Sioux were hunted and destroyed by the cavalry of Col. Phil Sheridan.)

Lost

*We danced in Dutch shoes and our tiny
hearts pounded to the clop-clop of
childhood's attraction.*

*We slowly made our way homeward
in the early years and exchanged valentines;
you stopped to talk while riding
your bicycle, and I caught my breath
at your red cheeked beauty.*

*We rode through the night with all
the boys and girls in the thrill of the
chill snow on the big sleds behind
the panting horses.*

*You turned in your desk in the
classroom to help me with that
penmanship exercise.*

*You came as a vision of radiant
loveliness in the classroom and you
signed my annual in high school.*

*We danced at the country club
when we were in college, and all the
men's eyes were following you.*

*We drove through the night high
up in the hills and there was
beauty all around us.*

*But you found your way
with another, we said goodbye.
I returned, and was lost.*

Myrtle and Della
A Story in Blank Verse

They were small town schoolmates
Sharing the choice secrets
    of little girls,
Myrtle, attractive and beautiful
Della, plain and shy.
Both were ecstatic
    about Jeff Dillon,
the school Apollo, and
shared their fantasies.

Then their paths divided;
Myrtle was swept off her feet
By the handsome visitor from the city.
Why wait for Jeff on the chance
He might propose?
Against her mother's caution,
She eloped with him.
Della was left with her dreams
Of Jeff who never called.

A year passed
And Myrtle returned to visit.
Della overwhelmed her with questions
About the exciting life,
But Myrtle confided she had
    wanted to come home.
Her mother had responded,
"You made your bed,
Now lie in it!"

While Della had imagined
The grand life of her friend,
Myrtle had imagined
The joy of the things she remembered
Things she was sure of.
But she found Jeff was married,
Little welcome at home.
Della was only sympathetic.

And the years went by,
Myrtle lost her first baby.
The second was a boy.
Her husband, restless, kept
*   the family moving.*
On one move they returned
To buy the old family home,
After her folks moved.
For a brief while it renewed old joys.

But her husband was seldom home
He was in the city on business,
On the move again.
Myrtle swung in the hammock
*   in the yard under the cherry trees*
Or she took her son
*   now in school,*
Across the river to visit
*   the grandparents.*

Across the years plain Della
Busied herself with housework
Had few gentlemen callers
None of whom proposed.
After her parents died,
There was little to do in the house;
She had been occupied with their care
But now during the long winters
She did some sewing and reading,
And in summer sat on the porch and rocked.

Myrtle long ago
Moved to the West Coast with her husband.
Her son had married. His wife
gave birth to a baby girl
And for the first time
she found life empty as the years
were for Della.
Again she thought of the old times
And pleasant days together.

When her husband died
she planned a trip East.
When summer came
She was on her way.
She visited all the old scenes,
Her old home next to Jeff Dillon's.
As she looked, he suddenly appeared!
She would recognize him anywhere,
Regardless of age or place.
Would he know her? She was rooted and still
as he walked past!

Myrtle felt very much alone
She walked back to the motel
And looked at the four walls
She needed to learn how to live
by herself; for the first time
she thought of Della's long experience.
Next day she joined Della
and neither was lonely.
They sat on the porch and rocked.

Preoccupied

The days are daying,
Bees are beeing,
Birds are birding,
Horses are horsing,
People are peopling,
All the world goes on worlding
Through time and space.

But the dark is darkening,
Bees are fleeing,
The flowers are fading,
Birds nests raiding,
People depeopling,
And the world is a time bomb.
Disaster comes apace!

In his book, *The Hollow Men,''* T.S. Eliot wrote, ''This is the way the world ends, not with a bang, but a whimper.'' Eliot was possibly wrong on both. It may end in a nuclear bang without a whimper anywhere.

What to do this Christmas

1. *Seek out and visit a forgotten friend.*
2. *Encourage youth.*
3. *Forgive an enemy.*
4. *Listen.*
5. *Be kind.*
6. *Laugh a little.*
7. *Laugh a little more.*
8. *Gladden the heart of a child.*
9. *Forego malice and envy.*
10. *Share your blessings.*

Then you will not be afraid of this Christmas season's mad pace. The first Christmas will appear with a strange new excitement, God's entrance into the world!

The Professor

There he stands
Brave little man,
Gladiator of the classroom.
As he looks out over his audience,
There's a gleam of satisfaction
In his practiced eye,
For they are novices,
And he is an old hand at this.

But where is his opponent?
Ah, that's the point!
He selects from memory at random,
And breathes his own breath
Into an idea to give it form;
He hypnotizes his auditors with believing
They see a gigantic opponent before him—

Socrates, Plato, Aristotle,
Descartes, Leibnitz,
These can't be there in person
To defend themselves.
This is a spot any ring veteran could dream about!
(But the obsession would put him away
under observation.)

The professor spars for an opening;
Today's opponent he gives top billing,
And he must not be off his guard.
He has built him up to tremendous proportion;
In fact he tells his audience
The opponent is God!
But he shows no fear
Of this anthropomorphism.

He climbs to the top of his desk
To reach and pummel the Deity
He claims is non-existent!
His auditors gaze in speechless wonder
At his audacity

Some laugh—some cry—
but few applaud—
One physics student tries to calculate
Why so much energy should be expanded
On a quixotic assumption,
But the professor continues
His relentless quarrel to the bell,
Caught in the web of his own thought.

At last he lies exhausted
Amid a welter of sprained brain cells
And his own blown tonsils—
The students leave the fetid classroom,
Break forth into the sunshine,
And wonder why the professor
does not follow—
Could it be he might see
His shadow and believe?

Prayer of Fulfillment

Our Father, we pray for the abundant living
which Jesus brought to earth—
Fill our bodies with thy health,
Fill our minds with thy wisdom,
Fill our wills with thy courage,
Fill our spirit with thy guidance,
Fill our community with thy love,
Fill our world with thy peace!

Silent at Sunset

Let me be silent at sunset
*   Let there be no outcry, no whisper,*
But as one starting on a long journey
*   Considers thoughtfully the way.*

In the evening of our life we shall be judged
by how we loved.

St. John of the Cross

Poetry of Jessie Wise

Jessie Wise's short lines are reminiscent of Japanese Haiku.

In Due Time

The Author wrote the play
You've only to portray
the part assigned
And mind,
A grace-full bow at curtain call.

Sunflowers

Sunflowers were painted by Van Gogh
They were beautiful before that
Though.

Winter

Winter drifted snows at will,
amassed a Kingdom and reigned until
a single robin on the wing
came for a crumb and sang of Spring.

Summer

Summer surrendered herself to Fall
without regret, for after all
with the last rose gone
and the sweetest nectar drawn,
Why go on?

Outside the Winner's Circle

When space is small and circumscribed,
there's only room for one inside.
No other one can come into
the guarded cell wherein I wait
and watch the race of men
through mirrored light, reflecting on
the glory won by men who choose to run and win
the race I did not enter in.

Nunc Dimittis

"Gentleman," —thus the professor—
"That will be all for today."
Business of shuffling and scuffling,
Putting of notebooks away;
Business of leaving the classroom,
Business of reaching the air,
Business of laughing and shouting,
Finding the out of doors fair.

Years have gone by; the professor,
Doddering, doting and grey,
Still tells philosophy classes,
"That will be all for today,"
Folds his worn notes in his pocket,
Wearily stumbles his way.
Over the dusk dreaming campus,
Watching the sunset's last ray,

Someday an angel will tap him
Soft on the shoulder and say,
"Mr. Scholastic Thompson,
That will be all for today."

Joseph MacDougall